THINKING CHRISTIAN WOMAN

HELEN HOSIER

HARVEST HOUSE PUBLISHERS
Eugene, Oregon 97402

THE THINKING CHRISTIAN WOMAN

Copyright © 1988 by Harvest House Publishers
Eugene, Oregon 97402

Library of Congress Catalog Card Number 87-0081656
ISBN 0-89081-612-3

Acknowledgments

They say a person is himself plus the food he eats, the books he reads and the friends he makes. I think that's true. My own thinking has been greatly enriched through the many fine books I've read and I deeply appreciate insights gleaned through the years from authors who have become spiritual mentors to me, including Dr. A. W. Tozer, Andrew Murray, Brother Lawrence, J. B. Phillips and Oswald Chambers. You will find me quoting them in this material. I am grateful for the rich legacy these writers have left us. Some are no longer living, but their contribution to the field of literature remains. I am also indebted to others who continue to expend the effort to provide food for thought, proving the truth of the maxim, "A drop of ink makes millions think."

And if perchance a fellow author recognizes something he or she may have said or written and it isn't acknowledged, please recognize that God used that bit of information and wisdom in my life, and I was blessed and helped by it so much that it became a part of me. Recently I was reading a book and parts of it sounded very familiar. Then I realized why. I thanked God that what He had given me at one time had become a blessing to someone else, and a part of their thinking.

That's what I pray will happen with the material in this book. I trust it will illuminate your thinking so much so that it becomes a part of you.

I've put off writing this book for years because there

was so much I wanted to say, and because I found myself gaining new insights into the Word of God and experiencing so much. How to distill it into something practical, manageable, motivational and inspirational loomed as an awesome task. Yet, now more than ever, I see the need for women to awaken to their tremendous potential. I thank all those who encouraged me in this undertaking.

In particular, I acknowledge with an ever-increasing awareness just how important those special people are who have intersected my life—loyal people who unfailingly expressed love and ongoing prayerful support—and who stood with me through some very difficult times: Anne Anderson, Marguerite Appling, Dorothy Casaccio, Kim Henschel, Eddie Huff, Barbara Johnson, Cheryl Koch, Hulda Liljegren, Gloria Rowe and Carol Rowland.

As usual, my acknowledgment of gratitude to my devoted husband; and the love and understanding of our children.

To editor Eileen Mason, thank you for wise counsel.

—Helen Hosier
Spring 1988

Contents

Introduction 🖋

I've read that in the course of a day, the average person will eat three-and-a-half pounds of food, speak 4,800 words and exercise 7 million brain cells. When I tell women that, it usually elicits a few gasps and startled responses. "Imagine eating that much food!"

We are greatly concerned about our bodies—counting calories and either losing weight or for sure not gaining any. While there is nothing inherently wrong with that concern, there is a growing need for us to expend the same amount of energy to push, stretch and exercise our minds. Rarely do we hear encouraging words or read much about nourishing one's mind to keep it in shape.

The flabby thinking among so many Christians, both men and women, gives cause for concern. The consequences can be devastating, and I suspect this lack of responsible thinking goes a long way to explain the condition of the church in the world today.

Beth Spring, contributing editor to *Christianity Today* magazine, points out the dearth of volumes addressing "our increasingly urgent need to 'think Christianly' " (Feb. 19, 1988). Indeed, few writers are addressing this area. Thus, the reason for this book.

We were in the Christian bookstore business in Southern California for several years. During that time I discovered there was a lot of Spirit-empowered thinking going on in the minds of Christian writers, and I was blessed and tremendously helped by their insights. Moreover, I found reading their books sent me into the pages of the Bible to search out the truths they called to my attention. I hungered for more. In the process of filling my mind with Christ-centered thoughts, I began to find it much easier to deal with the daily pressures of living.

I had loved the Bible and its familiar stories since I was a little girl. During that time of my life, however, as a young woman with a busy household and responsibilities in the bookstore business, the Bible came alive to me in a much more personal way. Christ became a living Savior to be followed and adored.

At the time I decided to do something about my new discoveries from the Word of God and from the writings of such inspired authors as Hannah Whitall Smith and Dr. A. W. Tozer. I began to seriously try to stretch my mind and practice the new principles I was learning. I remember Dr. Tozer asking the question, "Why, after years of Christian profession, do so many persons find themselves no farther along than when they first believed?" I had observed this situation many times while working in the Christian bookstore.

I am no longer in the bookstore business, but the conviction that the mind needs to be nourished, exercised and stretched has only become stronger through the years. I have come to see the mind as a fertile field. Cultivate it, plant good seed, nourish and water it, and it will produce magnificently.

Further, I don't see this as an option. I see it as something the Lord expects from those of us who call ourselves "Christian." Our response should be obedience. How much we need thinking Christian women in our world!

The Bible calls us to nurture three important attitudes in our minds: 1) alertness; 2) self-control; and 3) hopefulness. This is what the apostle Peter referred to when he said, "Prepare your minds for action; be self-controlled; set your hope fully on the grace to be given you when Jesus Christ is revealed" (1 Peter 1:13, NIV).

There is much despair and hopelessness all around us. How much we need minds filled with hope . . . to give purpose to living in the here and now and anticipation for the future. I call this "living with eternity's values in view." The thinking Christian woman demonstrates such a lifestyle, and the result is an emphasis on essentials.

The Bible also calls us to have the mind of Christ. This is possible through the power of the Holy Spirit working through us, yet so many Christians settle for less than best. I have a deep heart-longing to grasp the reality that as we think in our hearts, so we are (Proverbs 23:7). If we don't keep our thinking focused on God and the truths He has revealed to us, we won't have the mind of Christ nor the Holy Spirit at work in our lives. We will live unpeaceful, stress-filled lives.

Sometimes we get so busy making a living that we forget how to live. And our busyness breeds the dangerous tendency not to give time to cultivating and using our mental faculties. But as thinking Christian women we need to understand the wise use of time and the need to set and keep priorities. A thinking Christian woman has a well-defined value system.

Much has been said and written in recent years about the total woman, the sensuous woman, the sensitive woman, the fulfilled woman, and on and on it goes, challenging many of our perspectives. Some women have confided that certain books have given them a distorted view of God and what the Bible says about women; others have said they resented the implication they were to be manipulative, weak, submissive and subservient. "I'm really a strong person, and I'm a thinker," women have told me. "But I don't believe I'm domineering; I'm resourceful, a good worker..."

Then there are women who have told me that many things they've read and heard have tended to overwhelm them. In some instances they've come away with an inferiority complex. "I just can't measure up," they groan.

This book is the product of insights gained over many years, through personal reading, study and contacts with women from all walks of life and from all across the country. I don't intend for it to overwhelm you. We are not superwomen, and we are all prone to discouragement and disillusionment at times, both with ourselves and others.

Rather, I want to help you see the immense possibilities of your mind, to encourage you to be the woman in your heart of hearts you know you should and could be. I want to share some of what I've learned, to help each of us understand more clearly what it is God expects of us and how we can please Him.

Consider with me the many ways the thinking Christian woman can respond to all that life has to offer. Together let's seek to be thinking Christian women.

Part I

The Thinking Christian Woman Has the Mind of Christ

There is simply not enough time to think,
to become,
to perform what the constitution
of our nature indicates
we are capable of.
—A. W. Tozer[1]

But we have the mind of Christ.
—1 Corinthians 2:16

Who Is the Thinking Christian Woman? 🔥

> *But we have the mind of Christ.*
> (1 Corinthians 2:16)

The man is hunched over a crossword puzzle. The woman is engrossed in a book. He looks up at her and asks, "What's a five-letter word for hard-working, conscientious, reliable and durable?"

Without batting an eye she replies, "WOMAN!"

This cartoon makes us laugh. We like the answer and appreciate the self-confidence the woman demonstrates. She's obviously a thinking woman.

What do I mean by "a thinking woman"?

Is a "thinking woman" one who has a quick response, an agile mind? Is being clever, smart and sharp all there is to it? While those characteristics may adequately describe the thinking secular woman, that is, one who is not committed to following Christ (Romans 8:5-8), they only partially portray the thinking Christian woman. For she has something else going for her—something that undeniably sets her apart (vv. 9-17).

Simply defined, a thinking woman is one who cultivates and uses her mental faculties. The thinking *Christian* woman, however, understands that *all* of life must be lived in the context of being accountable to God. She

13

bases her choices, actions and words on what is God-honoring, and this perspective colors her entire life. To think as Christ would think is her goal.

The Mind of Christ

Thinking as Christ would means thinking biblically. The Bible says that if we are Christians, we have the mind of Christ (1 Corinthians 2:16). It also says we are to have renewed and transformed minds (Romans 12:2). But how does that actually take place?

The steps involved in this process are defined throughout God's Word. For example, it instructs us to look unto Jesus, the author and finisher of our faith (Hebrews 12:2), and diligently pursue holiness and peace with everyone, lest we fall short of the grace of God (vv. 14-15). Also, we are told to think on things above, not on earthly matters (Colossians 3:2).

The hymnist wrote, "Take time to be holy, the world rushes on; Much time spend in secret/With Jesus alone; *By looking to Jesus, Like Him thou shalt be*; Thy friends in thy conduct/His likeness shall see."[1] (Italics added.)

Cultivating a Christian perspective and response to life's issues results in a commitment to be and do what is pleasing to the Father. This requires a growing mind, one that is open, alert, and sensitive to God.

To be a thinking Christian woman, one must spend time *with* the Father, including *time in His Word*. Only then will her life reflect sound thinking—listening to and obeying the voice of God.

In contrast, the woman who is not committed to thinking like Christ reveals the poverty of her soul through attitudes and actions that are unbecoming to one who calls herself a Christian. Her relationships suffer; she doesn't have a well-defined value system. She has problems with her emotions, and doesn't know the meaning of true love nor the virtues of caring. She lacks discernment, can't control her tongue, doesn't know how to share her faith, is discontent and shows ingratitude. The fruit of the Spirit is not evident in her life.

Principle

The thinking Christian woman understands that to walk effectively with and for God she must develop the mind-set that says, "I can have the mind of Christ." But how do we develop such a mind-set? Where do we begin?

Developing a Right Mind-Set

It is incredible to think that mere mortals can have the mind of Christ. Yet the apostle Paul boldly stated, "But we have the mind of Christ."

In explaining this concept he wrote, "Let this mind be in you which was also in Christ Jesus; who, being in the form of God, did not consider it robbery to be equal with God, but made Himself of no reputation, taking the form of a servant" (Philippians 2:5-7).

Servanthood. God in the flesh was a servant. In Mark's gospel, Jesus said He did not come to be served, but to serve (Mark 10:45). John's gospel tells of when Christ laid aside His garment, took a towel and girded Himself, poured water into a basin and washed the disciples' feet (John 13:1-17) as an act of instruction. "For I have given you an example, that you should do as I have done to you . . . If you know these things, happy are you if you do them" (vv. 15, 17).

Having the mind of Christ also involves suffering. I don't think the apostle Peter ever forgot this. In his writings he talked about suffering patiently according to the will of God because "Christ also suffered for us, leaving us an example, that [we] should follow in His steps" (1 Peter 2:21). "Therefore, since Christ suffered for us in the flesh, arm yourselves also with the same mind" (1 Peter 4:1). We are to have the same thought, the same purpose in mind, the same attitude as Jesus.

In her book *Lord Change Me*, author Evelyn Christenson says the admonition to have the mind of Christ, whether in servanthood or suffering, is one of the awesome privileges of being God's child. "Whenever I'm in doubt as to how God wants me to change, I am always safe in praying for the mind of Christ," she says. "So often I'm aware that my attitude, reaction or thoughts are not Christ-like, but am not sure exactly what God wants to substitute for them. But I never ask amiss when I pray for *the mind of Christ*."[2]

Child-like but Not Childish

One day while Christ was on earth, his disciples began arguing among themselves as to who was going to be greatest in the kingdom of heaven. In the midst of the furor, Jesus silently motioned for a young child to come to Him. I can just picture Him wrapping His strong arms around that precious little one, and the child looking trustingly into the face of this kind Man. Then Jesus interrupted the argument and said, "Unless you change and become like little children, you will never enter the kingdom of heaven" (Matthew 18:3, NIV).

"Become *like* little children." The emphasis, I believe, must have been on becoming "like" them, with their innocence, dependence, eagerness to learn, honesty, simplicity, faith, abounding trustfulness and freedom from care. For "Childlikeness" strongly contrasts "childishness," which implies being petulant, spoiled and demanding our own way.

If we are to be thinking Christian women, we must be as teachable as a little child, yet mature in thought. That is our starting point.

As the apostle Paul instructed, "Do not be children in your thinking . . . but in your thinking be mature" (1 Corinthians 14:20, NAS). He also said, "When I was a child, I used to speak as a child, think as a child, reason as a child; when I became a man, I did away with childish things" (1 Corinthians 13:11, NAS).

When Jesus set that dear child in the midst of the disciples and called upon them to humble themselves and become as little children, he had you and me in mind—all of His children. As we come before God with a meek and child-like spirit, he will teach us the truths we need to function as thinking Christian women who have the mind of Christ and the indwelling Holy Spirit.

In his classic book, *The Inner Life*, author Andrew Murray says,

> All the infinities of God and the eternal world dwell in the Word as the seed of eternal life. And just as the full-grown oak is so mysteriously greater than the acorn from which it sprang, so God's words are but seeds from which God's mighty wonders of grace and power can grow up [in the soil—the heart—of the Christian where it has taken root].
>
> We should learn to come to the Word as little children. Jesus said, "Thou hast hid these things from the wise and prudent, and hast revealed them unto babes" (Luke 10:21). The

prudent and wise are not necessarily hypocrites or enemies. There are many of God's
own dear children, who, by neglecting to cultivate a childlike spirit, have spiritual truth
hidden from them and never become spiritual
[wo]men.[3]

The Key: Spiritual Wisdom Through the Spirit

The principle of having the mind of Christ is further
explained in 1 Corinthians 2:7-16, which speaks of having spiritual wisdom. That passage says our words can
be wise because they are from God who has sent His
Spirit, and it is His Spirit that searches out and shows us
God's deepest secrets.

Paul logically explains, "No one can really know what
anyone else is thinking, or what he is really like, except that person himself. And no one can know God's
thoughts except God's own Spirit. And God has actually
given us his Spirit (not the world's spirit)" (v. 11, TLB).

Paul adds that he is using the Holy Spirit's words to
explain the Holy Spirit's facts. "But the man who isn't
a Christian can't understand and can't accept these
thoughts from God, which the Holy Spirit teaches. They
sound foolish to him, because only those who have the
Holy Spirit within them can understand what the Holy
Spirit means. Others just can't take it in. But the spiritual
man has insight into everything, and that bothers and
baffles the man of the world, who can't understand him
at all" (vv. 14-16). Consequently, regardless of how intelligent a thinking woman might be, she can't know the
Lord's thoughts unless the Holy Spirit indwells her.

The Old Testament prophet Isaiah said God's thoughts
were higher than our thoughts (see Isaiah 55:8-9). At first

glance that statement may seem to contradict Paul's words. But Scripture shows that the factor that allows us to have the mind of Christ even though God's thoughts *are* higher than ours is the indwelling Holy Spirit. Through Him, we *can* bring our thoughts into harmony with God's.

Think on These Things...

Principle: The thinking woman understands that to walk effectively with and for God she must develop the mind-set that says, "I can have the mind of Christ." This requires that she recognize that mind-set involves servanthood and suffering, as well as being child-like and relying on the Holy Spirit for wisdom.

God's Word says, "But we have the mind of Christ" (1 Corinthians 2:16).

1. On a scale of 1 to 10, with 10 representing the ideal, how would you rate yourself as a thinking Christian woman?
2. Summarize what you understand from this principle. Ask and answer: How can I become the thinking Christian woman that God intends for me to be? What are my strengths? My weaknesses?

She Has a Renewed Mind 🔥

Be transformed by the renewing of your mind.
(Romans 12:2)

In his book *The Christian Mind: How Should a Christian Think?* author Harry Blamires says the doctrines we accept as Christians are either authoritative and binding or they are false. They are deserving of submission or of total neglect. "The Christian mind has an attitude to authority which modern secularism cannot even understand, let alone tolerate."[1]

Most men and women today are so far from thinking in a Christ-like manner that they have great difficulty combining two vital concepts as they determine their picture of God—the concept of love and the concept of power-laden authority. While Christians can understand how these two attributes unite in God's character, most of the secular world regards God as an unjust deity. But, as Blamires points out, "It is either the bowed head or the turned back."[2] There is only obedience or disobedience.

As Christians, we believe our reasoning powers come from God. They are one of His gifts to us, not anything we could manufacture for ourselves. To accept this is to acknowledge that our thinking *can* come under His control. As Blamires says, "Christian thinking is incarnational."[3]

--------------------------- ❀ ---------------------------

Principle

Appropriate responses and distinctly Christian thinking result when we have been transformed by the renewing of our mind.

--------------------------- ❀ ---------------------------

Needed: Mind Transplants

"A mind transplant is necessary for everyone. The incision is made by the will, and the transplant itself is performed by the Holy Spirit," says Bill Hull, author of *Right Thinking*.[4]

Hull goes on to say that while every believer has the potential for having the mind of Christ, the percentage who actually obtain that mind or meaningfully move in that direction is small.[5] Why is that true?

The apostle Paul says it is because we are conformed to the pattern of the world (Romans 12:2). He had a lot to say about the "old nature," the "carnal mind," and those "who walk according to the flesh" (Romans 8:5).

He explains it like this: "To be carnally minded is death, but to be spiritually minded is life and peace. Because the carnal mind is enmity against God" (Romans 8:6,7). The answer for the thinking Christian woman is to be controlled by her new nature, which results in a transformation and a renewing of the mind. "And do not be conformed to this world, but be transformed by the renewing of your mind" (Romans 12:2).

This passage contains both a negative, "Be not conformed," and a positive, "be ye transformed." It presents the age-old conflict between the spirit of this world and the Spirit of God contending for possession of our thinking and our very being. It requires a *daily* renewal of the inward man, and it may mean we seek that renewal many times in the course of a day. It points up the need for a *conscious* recognition that we can't do it on our own—that we must, with a deliberate act of the will, commit ourselves to a moment by moment walk with the Father, made possible by the Holy Spirit.

Making a Difference

"The world is perishing for lack of the knowledge of God and the Church is famishing for want of His Presence," wrote Dr. A. W. Tozer. Thinking Christian women possess the capacity to help bring about change in the world today. How? "The instant cure of most of our religious ills would be to enter the Presence in spiritual experience, to become suddenly aware that we are in God and that God is in us."

As author Andrew Murray says, to be filled with heaven, the life must be emptied of earth.[6]

But how do we practically achieve that status? If we are honest, we have to admit we are all too easily lured into the world's way of thinking. Emptied of earth? How many people do you know who are empty of earth? Whose thinking isn't colored by what's going on about them? Who aren't really almost compulsively involved with the world?

Most of us too easily accommodate ourselves to the world. Even in our most sincere efforts to make the Gospel appealing, we let the world into the church through adopting attitudes and priorities that demonstrate divided loyalties. Our lives are often marked by pride, materialism, hypocrisy and superficial relationships with each other and with God.

For a period of time while I was writing this book, my family and I lived in the heart of Silicon Valley in California. Yuppieland. Daily I watched as the newspaper, the evening news and my own experiences in rubbing shoulders with those who worked in the electronics industry revealed the intense upward striving. I observed that greed and lack of concern for others typified individuals enamored with their status and what their paychecks were buying for them.

I specifically recall a news story in which the chairman of one of Silicon Valley's largest computer firms said he viewed business as war. "When I attack, it's war. Anything that's in my way I push aside."

Yet I've seen similar attitudes in the church. Are we genuinely different? Often the only difference is that what we are comes masked in holy piety. False pretenders in the pulpits. Jesus called them the blind leading the blind (Matthew 15:14). And those sitting in the pews are often nothing but a reflection of what is standing before them Sunday after Sunday.

How many Christians do you know today who are hated by the world? One of the distinguishing characteristics of early Christians was their martyrdom (Hebrews 11:35-38). How blessed are we—really blessed because people have insulted us, persecuted and reviled us for our beliefs? (Matthew 5:10,11). Perhaps the apostle Paul was thinking about what some of those Christians were enduring when he said we were to offer ourselves up to God as living sacrifices (Romans 12:1). He even said that is "reasonable," and that when we do it, a mind transplant takes place (v. 2).

In *Right Thinking,* author Hull says the most vital matter in the Church today is its gray matter—how its members think. It is incredible to consider that the three-pound, jelly-like mound tucked beneath our skulls could be what is keeping the Church from functioning as it should. Yet *we are* the visible vehicles of God's action in the world. Until our thinking embraces a wholehearted allegiance to God and His Truth, we His Church will not be able to fully carry out His intended purpose.

The renewing Paul talks about gives way to an entirely different way of thinking, judging, deciding. It is what being a thinking Christian woman is all about.

This divine transformation, however, isn't a once for all occurrence. Jesus said He would send the disciples the Helper, meaning the Holy Spirit, and that He would enable them to speak and act as transformed individuals whose minds were being renewed daily.

Have you ever felt that you were living in two worlds? I have. When I've been in the presence of obvious wrongdoing, I have often felt separated from what was going on. At those times I know I've experienced God's protection; furthermore, the Bible teaches that angelic beings are surrounding me.

While writing this book, I experienced that special care, during a painful incident between myself and two co-workers on a temporary work assignment. One afternoon a woman in the office called another woman and myself into her office to explain how to operate the computer printer. It was a bit complicated and I said, "Just a moment, I need to get a pad and write this down."

The other woman said, "I'll get mine, my office is closer."

"Great," I responded, "How about typing the instructions and taping them on the front of the printer so we can all refer to them?" The three of us agreed this was a good idea.

The next morning I came to work early in order to be undisturbed as I tried the printer for the first time. When I got there, however, the instructions weren't posted. Not wishing to take any chances on fouling up the system, I left my computer disk with a note: "Would you mind printing this for me first thing as it's needed as soon as possible? Thanks."

Later, when I went back to pick up the printed material and the disk, the woman handed the disk to me and said, "Print your own disks from now on. You were given instructions yesterday."

"Oh," I said, "I did come in early to do that, but the instructions hadn't been posted and I didn't want to take any chances."

"What do you mean?" she asked sharply. "What are you talking about . . . printed instructions? You were told what to do, do it."

The woman in the adjoining office chimed in, "What are you talking about, Helen? Who said anything about typing out the instructions? I sure didn't."

The two of them started laughing. By now my heart was pounding, and I sent a telegram prayer upward: *"Oh, dear Father, this is so ridiculous! Help! Help! I need your help to handle this."*

"Girls," I said quietly, "either I am losing my mind or my hearing, and frankly, I don't think either has happened. We discussed this yesterday afternoon. You took the notes," I said looking at the one young woman. "And we agreed you'd type them and place them here on the printer."

"Isn't that interesting," she said, looking at the other

woman with a smirk that implied, "It worked! We finally got her!"

"Do you have any recollection of that conversation taking place?" she asked the first woman. Once again they laughed scornfully.

Immediately the words came to mind that the devil is a liar and that it is "Satan who fills the heart to lie" (Acts 5:3).

When I returned to my office, I found myself struggling to hold back the tears. I retreated quietly and quickly to the ladies room to regain control of myself. Then I cried out to God, *Dear Father, I can't handle much more of this.* And then I heard myself saying, "I can do all things through Christ who strengthens me" (Philippians 4:13).

I realized then that I had emerged from that hurtful encounter unscathed, though admittedly shaken. What had happened? The mind of Christ had gone to work for me. He came to my rescue. This is what can happen when we are thinking Christian women.

The two worlds we Christians inhabit, the spiritual and the natural, are both very real. We have no trouble recognizing the natural world around us—we are subject to human foibles and weaknesses, and the world exacts a toll in living. But we need to remember that as children of God we possess heavenly status as well, and we don't have to fight the battles in our own strength. When we forget our heavenly position, we become discouraged and disheartened. What is the answer for the thinking Christian woman?

A Thought "Conditioner"

A. W. Tozer said the truth must run in our blood and condition the complexion of our thoughts. "We must practice living to the glory of God, actually and determinedly. By meditation upon this truth, by talking it over with God often in our prayers, by recalling it to our minds frequently as we move about among men, a sense of its wondrous meaning will begin to take hold of us. The old painful duality will go down before a restful unity of life. The knowledge that we are all God's, that He has received all and rejected nothing, will unify our inner lives and make everything sacred to us."[7] Transformed thinking. Renewed minds.

I can tell you from experience that this concept works. Thinking women know all about the importance of right conditioners for body beauty. How much more so, then, should the thinking Christian woman be concerned about that which will give her the kind of mind-set that sets her apart and marks her as different.

The psalmist wrote that the wicked man does not seek God; God is in none of his thoughts (Psalm 10:4). God in our thoughts makes us different.

The following four steps are vital for the thinking Christian woman to understand if she is to develop the Spirit within:

1. *Meditate on the Word of God daily.*
   The power of God is passive in us until faith is exercised. Faith cometh by hearing the Word of God.

   "Search me, O God, and know my heart; test me and know my anxious thoughts. See if there is any offensive way in me, and lead me in the way everlasting" (Psalm 139:23-24, NIV).

   This humbling of ourselves before God, asking Him to search our hearts as we meditate on His Word, is powerful in making it possible for Him to reveal the Truth that renews and transforms.

2. *Practice the Word of God moment by moment.*
   Apply it to your every action and thought.

3. *Give the Word first place.*
   Make it a habit to ask yourself regarding situations that come into your life: "What would Jesus have me do? What does the Bible say?"

4. *Obey the voice of the Spirit.*
   God and the spiritual world are real. Become familiar with the voice of God. Pay attention to inner nudgings, to your conscience, to what the Bible says to you as you read and meditate on it. Listen to that voice through your spiritual mentors—other Christians you respect and trust, those you know are sensitive to the things of the Lord. God has many ways of getting our attention; pay close attention and be obedient.

Old, long-held habits do not die easily. Escaping the snares of the world will require intelligent thought and an exercise of aggressive faith. But it will be worth it.

Only to sit and think of God,
Oh what a joy it is!
To think the thought, to breathe the Name
Earth has no higher bliss.
—Frederick Faber

Think on These Things...

Principle: Appropriate responses and distinctly Christian thinking result when we have been transformed by the renewing of our mind.

God's Word says, "Be transformed by the renewing of your mind" (Romans 12:2).

1. Write out what being transformed by the renewing of your mind means to you. (Hint: Read Romans 8:5-10 for a description of the carnal mind. Ephesians 4:17-24 describes the "new [wo]man in Christ," and speaks of being renewed in the spirit of your mind.)
2. Romans 12:9-21 speaks of behaving like a Christian. List those behaviors and then evaluate yourself. Ask God to show you areas in your life and thinking that could use improvement.
3. We who follow Christ inhabit two worlds: the spiritual and the natural. On a scale of 1 to 10, with 10 representing the spiritual, in which "world" do you feel you spend most of your time? Explain your answer.
4. What do you consider "spiritual" acts? "Secular" or "natural" acts?
5. Is such compartmentalizing of our lives necessary? If not, why not? What is the answer?

She Is Spiritually Receptive and Aware 🦅

Be filled with the Spirit.
(Ephesians 5:18)

It has been my privilege to interview some of the great Christian women of our time for books I have written. When I have come away from spending time with such people as Morrow Graham (Billy Graham's mother), Josephine Johnson (mother of Wallace Johnson, dedicated Christian layman and co-founder of Holiday Inns International) and Mary Lee Bright (mother of Bill Bright, founder and president of Campus Crusade for Christ International), it has been with the sure sense that I have been in the presence of women who possessed spiritual sensitivity.

This spiritual awareness showed itself in their conversation and in their demeanor. Something in them was open to heaven.

Royal Resources

I recall Morrow Graham sitting in her living room with her hands folded serenely in her lap, saying, "The passage that has meant so much to me in the Bible is 2 Peter 1:3-9." She then recited it from memory:

According as His divine power hath given unto us all things that pertain unto life and godliness, through the knowledge of Him that hath called us to glory and virtue:

Whereby are given unto us exceeding great and precious promises; that by these ye might be partakers of the divine nature, having escaped the corruption that is in the world through lust.

And beside this, giving all diligence, add to your faith virtue; and to virtue, knowledge; And to knowledge, temperance; and to temperance, patience; and to patience, godliness; And to godliness, brotherly kindness; and to brotherly kindness, charity [love].

For if these things be in you, and abound, they make you that ye shall neither be barren nor unfruitful in the knowledge of our Lord Jesus Christ.

But he that lacketh these things is blind, and cannot see afar off, and hath forgotten that he was purged from his old sins (KJV).

There was a faraway look in her eyes as she spoke, as if she was remembering the strength and help those words had provided through many decades of living. "My burden for the women of the world is the same that Billy proclaims wherever he goes: that they will come to know Christ as their Savior, then get into Bible study and carry out the teachings of the Word of God in the daily experiences of their lives," she said.

I can still hear her repeating those words which had been a guiding light throughout her lifetime. It left an indelible impression. Her entire demeanor displayed an attitude of praise and adoration toward God.

Such a gracious southern lady. What was it that made Morrow Graham different? It was the "divine power" and "divine nature" the apostle Peter spoke of in these verses. She had cultivated spiritual receptivity and had acquired the habit of spiritual response. She was a thinking Christian woman.

Josephine Johnson was 91 years old when I visited her in Memphis, Tennessee. A wee mite of a woman with tiny wrinkled hands, she was the queen-lady of Rosewood Convalescent Center. The years had etched themselves into her happy face, and her eyes twinkled as she talked. Her countenance beamed with a peace and contentment that can only come from having lived secure in the knowledge that what had come to her was from the hand of God. "Recognize that in everything God has a purpose and He has a plan, and it will be better than the one you were working on," she emphasized as we talked. Her words rang with wisdom.

After talking with Mary Lee Bright in her Coweta, Oklahoma home, I carried with me the vivid memory of a quiet, self-effacing woman of God whose gentle spirit showed in the concern she expressed for women of today. "I have deep compassion for women who are complacent about life," she said. "If Christian mothers lived according to the teachings of the Word of God, they could change the world through their influence on the lives of their children," she told me.

These three women provided me with real-life demonstrations of being controlled by the Spirit, filled with the fullness of God. And the one vital quality they shared in common was spiritual receptivity. It was unmistakable.

--------------------- ---------------------

Principle

Spiritual awareness—receptivity and sensitivity to the Spirit of God—is the hallmark of the thinking Christian woman.

--------------------- ---------------------

Her inward longing to please God results in spiritual response. She recognizes that yearning is a gift from Him and she carefully nurtures it, knowing it can be increased by exercising responsiveness or destroyed by neglect.

Power in the life of a believer is always linked to the Spirit of God. The Bible speaks about the fruit of the Spirit, being filled with the Spirit, walking in the Spirit and being baptized in the Spirit.

What Does It Mean to Be "Filled with the Spirit"?

The apostle Paul urged his readers to "be filled with the Spirit" (Ephesians 5:18). It's not an option; it's a necessity.

In Colossians he explained, "For in Christ all the fullness of the Deity lives in bodily form, and you have been given fullness in Christ" (Colossians 2:9-10, NIV).

This is the certain and immediate inheritance of every child of God. However, it is in the practical outworking of our Christian experience that we decide and demonstrate whether we are going to allow the Spirit to have control. The thinking Christian woman's life is marked by choices that reveal spiritual receptivity and sensitivity.

Paul provides a four-way test to help us determine who is in control. Following his statement that we are to be filled with the Spirit, he says that to walk in the way of wisdom is to: 1) guard our speech; 2) sing (sensitive worship of God), and have an attitude of praise and adoration toward God; 3) give thanks; and 4) honor Christ by submitting to one another (Ephesians 5:19-21).

In other words, godly communication and a song in the heart are signs of Spirit-controlled living. Moreover, the absence or presence of an attitude of gratitude that trusts God in all circumstances (1 Thessalonians 5:18; Romans 8:28; James 1:2-4) and a willingness to nurture one's relationships give evidence of whether the Holy Spirit is in control.

The psalmist wrote, "I will sing to the Lord as long as I live. I will praise God to my last breath! May He be pleased by all these thoughts about Him, for He is the source of all my joy" (Psalm 104:33,34 TLB). It is not always easy to have a song in one's heart through the inevitable trying circumstances that come into our lives. But the thinking Christian woman, consciously walking in the Spirit and under His control, knows it is possible.

What Does It Mean to "Walk in the Spirit"?

We must recognize that the Spirit-filled life is not a sinless life. We still miss the mark. *Progress*, I often say, is a more appropriate descriptive word for the Christian life than perfection. (If this thought is perplexing, read 1 John 1:8 which says, "If we claim to be without sin, we deceive ourselves . . .") Galatians 5:16 directs us to "walk in the Spirit." As we do that, *consciously* seeking the mind of Christ, we will sin less and will bear spiritual fruit (5:22,23). That word *consciously* is the key. For the *conscious* choice we make will determine the *quality* of the fruit we produce.

The days of my husband's and my lives are filled with the activity that accompanies his position as an associate pastor and director of a Christian school. One of the more pleasurable pastimes we enjoy when we have a spare moment involves driving the back roads through the grape and fruit country in our part of California. Drinking in the beauty of those luscious grapes, row after row, mile after mile, and the fruit-bearing trees—peach, plum, cherry, apricot, apple—awakens a sense of awe within us. We marvel at God's creation. And we recognize that those grapevines and trees are fulfilling the purpose for which they were created.

I can't read the apostle Paul's description of what it means to be a fruit-bearing Christian without thinking of the juicy peaches we bought at the roadside stand, or those magnificent grapes sparkling in the sunlight. Something in me cries out to God, "Oh, dear Father, may my life produce the luscious fruits of love, joy, peace, longsuffering, kindness, goodness, faithfulness, gentleness and self-control. And I am reminded that it is the Holy Spirit who produces that in me (Galatians 5:22,23).

If the inner life is to be nurtured and the outer life is to give evidence of being under the control of the Holy Spirit, then we must seek to ever be spiritually receptive and sensitive.

> For this reason I bow my knees to the Father of our Lord Jesus Christ... that He would grant you, according to the riches of His glory to be strengthened with might by His Spirit in the inner man, that Christ may dwell in your hearts by faith; that you, being rooted and grounded in love, may be able to comprehend with all the saints what is the breadth and length and depth and height—to know the love of Christ which passes knowledge; that

you may be filled with all the fullness of God (Ephesians 3:14,16-19).

Think on These Things...

Principle: Spiritual awareness—receptivity and sensitivity to the Spirit of God—is the hallmark of the thinking Christian woman.

God's Word says, "Be filled with the Spirit" (Ephesians 5:18).

1. Complacency or control—Spirit-filled control. On a scale of 1 to 10, with 10 representing the ideal, where would you place yourself? Are you complacent about things of the Spirit, or are you consciously seeking to walk in the Spirit?
2. Explain your answer. Do some heart-searching. Try to identify what it is that may be keeping you from reaching the ideal. Some hindrances might be: failure to spend time reading the Bible; the busyness of your life; the need to be taught more about being filled with the Spirit, walking in the Spirit, and being controlled by the Spirit; the inability to integrate biblical principles into your lifestyle. There may also be others. Have you heard of the "barrenness of a busy life"? That is not uncommon for us as women to experience.
3. Are you producing the fruit of the Spirit? Here's a checklist. Honestly rate the quality of your fruit.

Superficial: Trying to live up to people's expectations. Thinking first of what people will say rather than what is pleasing to God.

Complacent: Little or no growth; self-satisfied; happy with the status quo.

Genuine: Sincerely or honestly felt or experienced; free from pretense.

	Superficial	Complacent	Genuine
Love			
Joy			
Peace			
Longsuffering			
Kindness			
Goodness			
Faithfulness			
Gentleness			
Self-control			

Part II

The Thinking Christian Woman Guards Her Thought Life

When the man [woman] becomes a thinking [wo]man a great deal has been accomplished. When the thinking [wo]man goes on to become a worshiping [wo]man a longer step has been taken toward full and perfect [wo]manhood. When the thinking, worshiping [wo]man has found his [her] hands and has put his [her] whole personality to work for the high honor of God and the blessing of mankind, some modest approach at least has been made toward Christlikeness and the restoration of the heavenly image ruined in the Fall.

—A. W. Tozer[1]

Fix your thoughts on what is true and good and right. Think about things that are pure and lovely, and dwell on the fine, good things in others. Think about all you can praise God for and be glad about.

—Philippians 4:8 TLB

She Abides in Her Heavenly Father 🔥

> *Don't worry about anything; instead, pray about*
> *everything; tell God your needs and don't forget to*
> *thank Him for His answers. If you do this you will*
> *experience God's peace, which is far more wonderful*
> *than the human mind can understand. His peace*
> *will keep your thoughts and your hearts quiet and at*
> *rest as you trust in Christ Jesus.*
> (Philippians 4:6,7, TLB)

One morning before leaving for work I called my daughter. In the background I heard her 3-year-old daughter Christa crying. "Christa sounds unhappy," I commented.

"Yes," my daughter replied, "she didn't get to tell her daddy good-bye. They have this little morning ritual. She loves the hugs and kisses, and so does he."

That prompted my thinking as I drove to work. This precious child loves her father so much she wants to start the day by letting him know it. Moreover, there is something about the love she receives from him that is important to her throughout the day.

God has unique ways of teaching us. In my case, He often uses little children. That day He showed me how He *wants* to bless us, how He is waiting for us to reach up

41

to Him each morning and say, "Good morning, Father, I love You..."

----------------------------------- ❦ -----------------------------------

Principle

The thinking Christian woman seeks to live in unbroken fellowship with her heavenly Father. She abides in Him (John 15:1-11).

----------------------------------- ❦ -----------------------------------

When our children are little, we teach them to say goodnight prayers. I cherish memories of kneeling alongside the children by their beds and listening to them pray, praying with them.

I also remember how my mother knelt with me when I was a child. That habit has stayed with me so that as an adult I still talk to the Father before I fall asleep. In fact, some of my best times for prayer are the uninterrupted bedtime hours—often when sleep won't come or when I awaken in the middle of the night.

I discovered years ago, however, as a busy young mother, that prayer at night wasn't enough. I learned I needed to turn my thoughts to the Father immediately upon awakening. The busyness of the day—getting the children up, dressed, fed, and off to school, as well as all the other matters needing my attention—overwhelmed me. I came to realize that what I needed was unbroken fellowship with the Father. I needed inner fortification to face the demands of the day. I needed to take up where I left off the night before in my praying. That discovery began for me the morning watch, "Father, thank You for the night's rest, for keeping watch over us while we slept. Now, dear Father, go with us into this new day. I need your help . . ." There were many mornings when all I could say was, "Oh dear Father, help!" Believe me, the Father understands such cries. Many times He reminded me, "My child, you can overwhelmingly conquer through Me" (Romans 8:37).

This principle of having a morning watch was Andrew Murray's secret to the close, intimate walk He experienced with the Lord. He called it the keynote of his daily life. "It is this fixed decision to secure Christ's presence . . . [that] will make the morning watch itself a mighty force in strengthening our character and giving us boldness to resist self-indulgence," he said.

Maintaining the Glow All Day

Murray points out, however, that the transition from fellowship with God in the morning hour to interaction with our fellow men is often difficult. Going to the kitchen to fix breakfast is often proof of that!

How easy it is to lose that sense of God's Presence when we are confronted with demanding others. I've said on occasion that the devil can wear a familiar face. Sometimes the place where we work is very difficult. Whether it's our husbands, employers, employees, coworkers, friends or our children who present a challenge—how do we maintain the glow?

The account of Moses coming down from the mountain after his encounter with God (Exodus 34:29-30,33), and of the glow on his face, teaches an *important* lesson. *Close and continued fellowship with the Father should leave its mark on us.*

In his letter to the Christians at Corinth, Paul discusses this idea and specifically mentions the glory that was revealed in Moses' face. He asks an important question,

"Now if the old administration held such heavenly, though transitory, splendour, can we not see what a much more glorious thing is the new administration of the Spirit of life? If to administer a system which is to end in condemning men had its glory, how infinitely more splendid is it to administer a system which ends in making men right with God! . . .

"With this hope in our hearts we are quite frank in our ministry. We are not like Moses who veiled his face to prevent the Israelites from seeing its fading glory. *But it was their minds really which were blinded . . . For the Lord to whom they could turn is the Spirit, and wherever the Spirit of the Lord is, men's souls are set free.*

"*But all of us who are Christians have no veil over our faces, but reflect like mirrors the glory of the Lord. We are transformed in ever-increasing splendour into His own image, and this is the work of the Lord who is the Spirit*" (2 Corinthians 3:7-18, Phillips, italics added).

How can we have unbroken fellowship with the Father? How can our lives demonstrate His glorious Presence? How can we have the power of Christ resting on us all day long? How do we maintain the glow?

Holy Watchfulness

Unbroken fellowship takes place as we *consciously* maintain a spirit of watchfulness. The Father has promised and we can claim His watchcare. Paul wrote,

> Be anxious for nothing, but in everything by prayer and supplication with thanksgiving let your requests be made known to God. And the peace of God, which surpasses all comprehension shall guard your hearts and your minds in Christ Jesus (Philippians 4:6,7 NAS).

The wisdom in Proverbs teaches:

> Watch over your heart with all diligence, For
> from it flow the springs of life (4:23).

These passages speak of unbroken communication with the Father—an awareness of His indwelling Presence and the need to stay in touch with Him. How do we achieve that? We have been given the means. Access to the Father is as simple as opening our lips in prayer, our ears to listen to what He is saying and our hearts to respond. It doesn't depend on posture or place. God hears *all* prayers.

The Branch Life

"Abide in Me," Jesus said, "Abide in My love" (John 15:4-10). When we do, we have His promise of unbroken fellowship.

What does it mean to "abide"? Andrew Murray wrote this about growing into Jesus the Vine, "Do not expect to abide in Him unless you will give Him that time . . . Come, my brethren, and let us day by day set ourselves at His feet, and meditate on this word of His, with an eye fixed on Him alone. Let us set ourselves in quiet trust before Him, waiting to hear His holy voice—the still small voice that is mightier than the storm that rends the rocks—breathing its quickening spirit within us, as He speaks: 'Abide in Me.' "

My Friend Anne Anderson had a growing gerontology practice in Sunnyvale, California. She was being used in a wonderful way to meet the needs of the aging and help families through the transition of separating beloved older family members from the familiar into surroundings where they could receive the care they needed. It was an amazing work, almost a pioneer effort since so little is actually being done when you consider the longevity that we now have in our culture.

And then Anne was stricken with not one, but three life-threatening illnesses. She had to learn to "let go" of many things, as she puts it. With much pain and deepest sorrow she let go of her practice, her university teaching position, her independence, her and her husband's life-style of gracious entertaining and even her sense of worth. She went through what has been called "the dark night of the soul," a "death of self" to God. All the known props and supports were gone. At times she felt abandoned even by God. But as she surrendered herself to Him, something beautiful began to happen.

As she found herself with enormous amounts of time —time she'd never had before—she began to get a glimpse into her own soul. Lying on the floor in her home overlooking the Pacific, in intense pain and anguish, Anne began to experience a union, a oneness with God unlike anything she'd ever experienced before.

As she explains it, "I was starved for this nourishment for my soul. When I am well—and I know I will be well again—I will never give up this practice of spending this kind of alone-time with the Father. I value this solitude. I know now I could never exist again without it."

The relationship between Jesus and those who would be His followers is like that of a vine and its branches. He is the true source of all life and spiritual vigor. Disciples of any age are entirely dependent on Him, just as branches are to the parent stem. So the condition for spiritual usefulness and maximum fruitbearing is identical with the natural one—abiding in the vine. When a good branch is severed from the vine, it will produce nothing, even though it was good. Union with Christ, the true Vine, is incomparably necessary to that one who hopes to bring forth fruit. "Apart from me," Jesus said, "you can do nothing."

The Father: Our "Pruner"

We must realize that the "vine life" also involves sometimes painful "pruning" in our lives. For while Jesus said He was the true vine, His "Father is the husbandman" (John 15:1). This means that the Father is watching over our abiding, our growth and our fruit bearing.

Jesus said, "Every branch in Me that beareth not fruit He taketh away: and every branch that beareth fruit, He purgeth it, that it may bring forth more fruit" (John 15:2). It is for fruit in our lives that the Husbandman, our Father, cleanses the branches.

We Californians know how vinedressers have to cut away dead wood. It is amazing to see how they prune back those magnificent vines. The dead wood—wild wood—needs the pruning knife because it draws away the strength and life from the vine, hindering the flow of sap to the grapes. The wood of those branches must decrease so the fruit of the vine may increase.

Likewise, we as children of God are heavenly branches. There is in our lives that which seems perfectly good and even legitimate, and yet draws away our interest and strength for the things of God. It must be pruned, cleansed and cut away. How easy it is to let the objects and cares of this world possess and overpower us.

During my conversation with Morrow Graham, she told me John 15:3 shows that the Father, as Husbandman, uses the pruning-knife of His Word to trim the "dead wood" from our lives. We can't do that for ourselves. We have to trust Him to do it for us. God *will* generate all that is necessary for our spiritual growth and full productivity if we abide in Christ, the true Vine, the root and source of all our help and hope.

One Step at a Time

There are a lot of people who are like Charlie Brown's friend Lucy. She tells him, "Life is difficult, isn't it, Charlie Brown?"

He answers, "Yes, it is."

Then she responds: "But I've developed a new philosophy. I just dread one day at a time."

I've got news for the likes of Lucy. We don't have to dread one day at a time. We can *take life* a step at a time. When we do, we can be confident God is ordering our steps as well as our stops. The Bible says, "The steps of a good man are ordered by the Lord, and He delights in his way. Though he fall, he shall not be utterly cast down; For the Lord upholds him with His hand" (Psalm 37:23,24).

Unbroken fellowship with the Father. Do you want it? Take the first step. Make time for Him upon arising each morning.

Think on These Things . . .

Principle: The thinking Christian woman seeks to live in unbroken fellowship with her heavenly Father. She abides in Him (John 15:1-11).

God's Word says, "Don't worry about anything; instead, pray about everything; tell God your needs and don't forget to thank Him for His answers. If you do this you will experience God's peace, which is far more wonderful than the human mind can understand. *His peace will keep your thoughts and your hearts quiet and at rest as you trust in Christ Jesus*" (Philippians 4:6,7, TLB, emphasis mine).

1. What does "abiding in Christ" mean to you? (Read John 15:1-11.) Why is it so essential to abide in Him?

What benefits are yours when you abide? What happens when you don't abide in Him?

2. Is this principle of living in unbroken fellowship with the Father new to you? If so, how are you going to put it into practice? How will you know that you are abiding in Him? (See also John 8:31,32.)

3. In what way does your relationship with God need strengthening? What do you think the results will be?

4. Read and reflect on these Scriptures: Psalm 62:1, 5-8; Psalm 63:1-8. Write down your thoughts, the mental pictures that come to mind. What are some of your favorite Scriptures that speak about the importance of abiding in the Father and of maintaining unbroken fellowship with Him?

She Nourishes Her Mind

> *Whatever is true, whatever is honorable, whatever is right, whatever is pure, whatever is lovely, whatever is of good repute, if there is any excellence and if anything worthy of praise, let your mind dwell on these things.*
>
> (Philippians 4:8, NAS)

It was said in ancient Israel that if a drop of ink fell at the same time on your book and on your coat, clean first the book and then the garment. In this fast-paced world in which we live, however, too few people share that degree of enthusiasm about books—especially books that make you think and books with a solid Christian emphasis.

Perhaps one of the reasons I like the apostle Paul so much is because he was a reader. In his last letter to Timothy, written while Paul was imprisoned and exiled from the work to which he was so dramatically called, he asked him to "Bring the books, especially the parchments" (2 Timothy 4:13b).

What was Paul referring to? The parchments were the sacred manuscripts, the copies of Scripture. However, the meaning of "the books" is not clear. We don't know what he was reading, but Paul was obviously a reader.

There are many Christians today who, like Paul, are

51

prisoners. But, unlike Paul, their imprisonment is self-imposed. Because they choose not to read, they are exiled from the good things to be had in the Christian life. With little or no exposure to that which can help them in their spiritual growth, they are stunted, weak, ineffective and uncommitted. Relying primarily on the spoon feedings they receive in Sunday morning church services, they remain babes in the faith, malnourished spiritually. For regardless of how good such feedings may be, spoon feedings for an infant would not keep him alive and healthy for long. This analogy carries over into our need for the milk of the Word and solid food as adult Christians.

Many believers' neglect of study of the Bible and past and contemporary thought as found in Christian literature shows itself in preference for "things" and entertainment. If they were ever to experience an actual imprisonment such as Paul endured, they might write a letter which would read, "Bring me the daily papers, the stereo, a Walkman or the radio, some goodies to eat, but especially a television. And, oh yes, if possible, smuggle in a VCR and some movies."

Principle

The thinking Christian woman guards her thought life and nourishes her mind. She recognizes that the mind and heart need the stimulation that comes as a result of carefully choosing and thoughtfully reading good literature. She especially recognizes the importance of studying the Word.

When I was in the Christian bookstore ministry, I heard many excuses as to why people don't read. One day I sat down and tried to sum them up. I decided I could safely boil them down to three: 1) I don't have time; 2) Books cost too much; and 3) I'm not a reader.

Let's look at those excuses.

1) I don't have time.

Books nourish the mind. If the inner life of devotion is to be fed and the outer life of service is to be guided, then good reading habits are essential. If one is too busy to keep spiritually fit, one is, indeed, too busy. I've observed that most people usually find time to do the things they really want to do. "I don't have time," is generally not a valid reason for not reading.

2) Books cost too much.

Just because haircuts have gone up from 25 cents to $6 or far more (depending on where you go), men and women haven't given up haircuts have they? Or gas— what did we used to pay for a gallon of gas? Remember those days? But we haven't given up driving cars. And what about clothing? Is our vanity such that we are willing to spend great sums on our outward selves but unwilling to spend anything on that which will enrich our personalities and nurture our inner person?

3) I'm not a reader.

Any habit worth developing is worth working at. Reading is a habit that takes time to cultivate if you aren't a natural-born book lover. Do you play golf? Exercise at the gym regularly? What is it you like and that you do well and wouldn't think of giving up? Did you do well at golf initially? Did you become an expert at crewel or needlepoint overnight? Are your skills as a gourmet cook the result of a day or two of cooking?

It Takes Time to Keep Spiritually Fit

I am often asked, "How do you find the time to read?" Usually the question is posed in such a way that I get the impression the person hopes I have some marvelous secret I can share with them.

The Bible says, "Take time and trouble to keep yourself spiritually fit" (1 Timothy 4:8 Phillips).

When do *I* read? How can *you* find the time to read? It is not a matter of "when" or "how." It's not *if we can find the time, but as we take the time to keep ourselves spiritually fit.* It is easy to overlook the fact that what goes into the mind, via literature or any other medium, profoundly affects our thinking. Substandard reading material, or little or no reading, is bound to result in substandard thinking and living.

A. W. Tozer said, "The reading habits of the average evangelical Christian in the U.S. are so wretchedly bad as actually to arrest his spiritual development and block the progress of the faith he professes to hold."

Eyes have been opened, hearts melted and life-changing decisions made through the pages of books. I recall asking a man if he had read a certain book. His answer? "Yes, I read it, and I felt it, too!" Such feelings are bound to produce action that has its effect not only in the life of the one acting, but in the lives of others around him as well.

Henry David Thoreau said, "A truly great book teaches me better than to read it. I must soon lay it down and commence living on its hint. What I began by reading, I must finish by acting." Certainly the best book is not one that merely informs, but one that stirs the reader to do something with what he has read.

A great philosopher once said, "My mind is myself. To take care of myself is to take care of my mind."

Author Howard Hendricks notes, "One of the most crucial means of stretching your mind is through the process of reading. The mind is like a muscle. It develops with use. You won't wear it out. No one ever dies with a brain that has been totally used. That will never happen. Though you do need to constantly stretch your mind, be careful what you feed it, because what you feed it will largely determine what you are."

There is awesome power in our mental processes. During the last days of World War II, someone commented to President Truman that he appeared to be bearing up quite well under the stress and strain. He answered, "I have a foxhole in my mind."

Cultivate the Art of Thinking by Reading

If another beatitude were to be added to those Christ gave I think I'd suggest, "Blessed be the lovers of books and those who feel the need to read."

When I go into people's homes, one of the first things I do is glance around to see what they are reading. I am saddened when I don't see good books. A house without books is like a room without windows. I feel sorry for children who grow up in a home where the parents are not readers, because example is vastly important. If the reading habits of Christians are to improve, Christian parents must take a look at themselves and ask, "What does my example say to our children?"

Someone wrote that we are a generation of spoonfed Christians, grown men and women wrapped in intellectual swaddling clothes who know more about bombs than the Bible, who talk more about counting calories than Christ. Our predecessors would have given their eyeteeth to have the superabundance of Christian literature and good books available today.

We sit back, yawn impolitely in the face of a thought-provoking book and choose to watch television. Lest that comes off sounding too harsh, it is generally acknowledged that television makes us very passive, which is certainly not conducive to the encouragement of an active, thinking mind.

Perhaps there are a few "secrets" that can help you to inch in some reading time. There's nothing revolutionary about these ideas, but they've worked for me.

1. Take an inventory of your time for a couple days. You will probably be amazed at the amount of time that is wasted. Begin to use that "wasted time" for reading.

2. Salvage minutes. Sandwich reading time into the busyness of your days. If you are a working woman, read on your lunch hour. If you use public transportation, read on the way.

3. Keep books and booklets on hand at all times. Never be without something to read. I used to squeeze in a lot of reading while waiting to pick up my children from Little League practice or piano lessons. Read at the beauty shop. Read in the bathroom. Read wherever and whenever you have an opportunity!

4. Take the Word of God seriously. Jesus said, "Have you never read . . . ?" (Mark 2:25). The apostle Paul said, "Give attention to reading, to exhortation, to doctrine . . . Meditate upon these things; give yourself wholly to them; that thy profiting may appear to all" (1 Timothy 4:13,15).

What Should You Be Reading?

At the top of your reading list should be the Bible. Bible-reading time, however, should not just be squeezed in as you find a few spare moments. It is vital that we spend *quality time* meditating in the Word. Ben Gurion said: "We have preserved the Book and the Book has preserved us."

When it comes to reading materials other than the Bible, sound choices are essential. Since what we read in a real sense enters the soul, it is vitally important that we read the best and nothing but the best. How can you be sure your reading outside the Scriptures meets that criterion?

A spiritual mentor can be a great help in this area, someone whose judgment you trust. Your pastor should be such a person, as well as Bible teachers, writers and others. Get their recommendations or have them comment on what you select. If you have a Christian bookstore nearby, use the staff as a resource. Subscribe to Christian magazines, or join a Christian book club.

There is one secular magazine I want to call to your attention because I believe it is worth reading. It is the *Saturday Evening Post*. Its editor and publisher, Dr. Cory SerVaas, is a dedicated Christian medical doctor and lay woman. As she grew up on an Iowa farm, she knew she wanted her life to count. God gave her an active mind and a strong belief in and reliance on His providence. The *Post* is a strong testimony to her faith and convictions.

Never, however, substitute reading Christian books or magazines for reading the Bible. Read God's Word first. Have you become familiar with some of the new paraphrases and translations? Ask your local Christian bookstore clerks to tell you about them. They will be glad to introduce you to *The New International Version* (NIV), the *New American Standard* (NAS), *The Living Bible* (TLB) and *The New King James* (NKJ). (These are the most familiar and best-selling of the new paraphrases and translations.)

Master the Bible and let it master you. The new translations and paraphrases can help.

No matter what you read, read to absorb. Read to learn. Read to apply. For as John Locke said, "Reading furnishes our mind only with materials of knowledge. It is thinking that makes what we read ours."

Reading Stretches and Equips You Spiritually

"Wear the old coat; buy the good book."

That old proverb is worth heeding. Consider what reading does for you:

1. It deepens your understanding of spiritual truth.

   When events in your life threaten to knock you off balance, being firmly grounded in spiritual reality enables you to say to yourself, "This is what the apostle Paul [or Peter, James, etc.] meant. Yes, I can handle this. Paul said not to be anxious, but by prayer and supplication with thanksgiving, to let my requests be made known to God, and He would give me His peace. *Father, give me that peace, that settled feeling in my heart that You are in control...*" We can be a testimony to others as they observe our Godly reactions to the difficult times in our lives.

2. It deepens your faith, devotion and love.

   The Word of God stored in our hearts is a reservoir of sustaining strength. We can stand strong when our faith is tried. God's Truth enables us to be loving to the unlovable, forgiving of that which is difficult to forgive.

3. Your heart is enlarged to share your Lord.

   From the overflow of our faith, we are able to share God's faithfulness and love.

4. Your testimony and service are more effective.

   Reading the testimonies of others and learning

how they dealt with the difficulties in their lives enables us to grasp onto hope. Thus, our own lives are more effective.

5. You will be aware of what to give others who have spiritual needs.

   When our 37-year-old neighbor's husband died of a massive heart attack during a bicycle marathon, I was able to go to my books on death and loss and give her material that was very helpful. I also knew where to direct her in the Bible for comfort.

6. You can use books to explain how to become and/or grow as a Christian.

   Campus Crusade (Here's Life Publishers), the Navigators (NavPress), Moody Bible Institute (Moody Press), InterVarsity Press and many other publishers have Bible study materials, small books and booklets and all kinds of printed helps for seekers, new Christians and for those who want to deepen their spiritual understanding.

7. Reading will help you find answers to life's questions.

   The Bible and Christian books teach and illustrate how to overcome temptation and how to know God's will. There is scarcely a subject you could think of that isn't somehow addressed in Christian writings. Christian writers are very contemporary with present-day needs. There is no excuse for ignorance in this day and age.

8. Finally, reading equips you to be a thinking Christian.

   A bulletin board in one of our church schoolrooms displayed children's responses to why they loved God and the Bible. These two caught my attention:

   I love God for giving me a brain. I could die from not knowing what a red light means.

I love God's way for making me smart. (This child had drawn a picture of a big Bible.)

These students captured the essence of what reading equips us to be. For reading Christians are growing Christians, and growing Christians are witnessing Christians. Reading prepares us for sharing from the overflow of our hearts. The thinking Christian woman recognizes how vital this quality is if she is to be maturing and effective in her faith.

Think on These Things...

Principle: The thinking Christian woman guards her thought life and nourishes her mind. She recognizes the mind and heart need the stimulation that comes as a result of carefully choosing and thoughtfully reading good literature. She especially recognizes the importance of studying God's Word.

God's Word says, "Fix your thoughts on what is true and good and right. Think about things that are pure and lovely, and dwell on the fine, good things in others. Think about all you can praise God for and be glad about" (Philippians 4:8, TLB).

1. Are you guarding your thought life and nourishing your mind? On a scale of 1 to 10, with 10 being the highest, where would you place yourself?
2. How many Christian books have you read in the last six months? In the last three months? In the last month? What are you reading now? Does it meet the criteria established by the Word of God to "fix your minds on whatever is true and honorable and just and pure and lovely and admirable" (Philippians 4:8, Phillips).

3. What steps are you going to take to devote yourself to daily, diligent study of the Word, and to a time of keeping yourself spiritually fit through reading and quiet meditation?

In his thought-provoking book, *New Testament Christianity*, J. B. Phillips says it is a profound mistake to suppose the Holy Spirit ceased to inspire writers when the New Testament was completed.

"There are many Christians today who from one year's end to another never read a Christian book. They have little or no idea, for example, how Christianity is spreading throughout the world, of the triumphs and disappointments of the world-wide Church . . . they are even hazy about the real and solid achievements of Christian men and women through the centuries. To be brutally frank, they are very ignorant both of the history and of the implications of their Faith. In other departments of life they may be highly competent, efficient and knowledgeable; but over this, the very heart and centre of their true life, they are frequently abysmally lacking in knowledge and awareness. These are, I know, harsh words, but the Church could be infinitely more powerful as God's instrument for the establishment of His Kingdom if its members were better informed in their minds as well as more devoted in their hearts."[1]

I want to challenge you. Consider taking the message of this chapter to the people in your church, Sunday school class, women's group or wherever you feel it may be needed. Ask God to give you wisdom. Speak to your pastor about this if you feel so inclined, but don't let the needed message lie dormant in your heart. Do something with it as a thinking Christian woman. Do it as unto the Lord.

Part III

The Thinking Christian Woman Has a Well-Defined Value System

God has set eternity in our hearts and we have chosen time instead. He is trying to interest us in a glorious tomorrow and we are settling for an inglorious today. We are bogged down in local interests and have lost sight of eternal purposes. We improvise and muddle along, hoping for heaven at last but showing no eagerness to get there, correct in doctrine but weary of prayer and bored with God.

—A. W. Tozer[1]

How completely satisfying to turn from our limitations to a God who has none. Eternal years lie in His heart. For Him time does not pass, it remains; and those who are in Christ share with Him all the riches of limitless time and endless years.

—A. W. Tozer[2]

Redeem the time (Ephesians 5:16).

She Lives with Eternity
in View 🔥

Live life, then, with a due sense of responsibility,
not as [wo]men who do not know the meaning of life,
but as those who do. Make the best use of your time,
despite all the evils of these days.
(Ephesians 5:15,16, Phillips)

I once heard the story of a very rich woman who had watched her pennies closely for years and invested wisely. When she died, she was worth several million dollars. Everybody in the small town where she had lived wondered exactly how much she had left, and one brave soul actually went to the woman's pastor and asked.

The pastor answered abruptly, "All of it."

He wasn't just being facetious. She *did* leave it all—every last cent, as all of us will.

Money, however, isn't the only valuable item people tend to hoard and leave. The most common resource we hoard is our lives.

We tend to relegate our talents, abilities and expressions of love and concern to the storage rooms of our lives. In many ways, we postpone living.

It has been said that Elizabeth, Queen of England, cried on her deathbed, "Millions of money for an inch of time." She had the wealth of a great kingdom at her disposal, but not one penny of it could buy her an added moment of time.

When he was just a little tyke, my son Kraig surprised me one day by asking, "Mom, is God letting us breathe?" My answer to him was a solemn one—a simple but sure reminder that every breath we take is given to us by God, for which we must be aware and thankful.

The Bible emphasizes the brevity of life and the need to make the best possible use of time. Ephesians 5:15,16 calls us to live with a due sense of responsibility, not as those who don't know the purpose and meaning of life, but as those who do. "Make the best use of time," we are told. "Redeem the time."

James 4:14 says, "How do you know what will happen even tomorrow? What, after all, is your life? It's like a puff of smoke visible for a little while and then dissolving into thin air" (Phillips). "What you ought to say is, 'If the Lord wants us to, we shall live and do this or that . . .' " (v. 15, TLB).

---------------------------------- ----------------------------------

Principle

Because the thinking Christian woman has a well-defined value system, she lives with eternity's values in view. Jesus said, "Watch therefore, for you do not know what hour your Lord is coming" (Matthew 24:42).

---------------------------------- ----------------------------------

Many believers today won't allow themselves to think about death and dying because, as one man told me, "It's too morbid." Morbid? Apparently he hasn't thought about what heaven is like.

The Bible, however, isn't silent about death and dying. It repeatedly shows that Christians don't have to dread what lies beyond death. The thinking Christian woman knows that to be absent from the body is to be present with the Lord, for this is what the Word of God teaches. As 2 Corinthians 5:1-9 explains,

"For we know that when this tent we live in now is taken down—when we die and leave these bodies —we will have wonderful new bodies in heaven, homes that will be ours forevermore, made for us by God himself, and not by human hands. How weary we grow of our present bodies. That is why we look forward eagerly to the day when we shall have heavenly bodies which we shall put on like new clothes. For we shall not be merely spirits without bodies. These earthly bodies make us groan and sigh, but we wouldn't like to think of dying and having no bodies at all. We want to slip into our new bodies so that these dying bodies will, as it were, be swallowed up by everlasting life. This is what God has prepared for us and, as a guarantee, He has given us his Holy Spirit.

Now we look forward with confidence to our heavenly bodies, realizing that every moment we spend in these earthly bodies is time spent away from our eternal home in heaven with Jesus. We know these things are true by believing, not by seeing. And we are not afraid, but are quite content to die, for then we will be at home with the Lord. So our aim is to please Him always in everything we do, whether we are here in this body or away from this body and with Him in heaven (TLB).

In comforting His disciples before leaving them, Jesus said, "Let not your hearts be troubled; you believe in God, believe also in Me. In My Father's house are many mansions; if it were not so, I would have told you. I go to prepare a place for you.

"And if I go and prepare a place for you, I will come again and receive you to Myself; that where I am, there you may be also" (John 14:1-3).

"Out of the mouth of babes . . ."

When my mother died in 1968, my youngest child was seven years old. He and his grandmother had been very close, and I was concerned about how her death would affect him. How was I to explain that Grandma Hattie would no longer be around to play with him and to take care of him?

I did my best to prepare him before we arrived at the funeral home. When we arrived, the room was already full of family and friends. We approached the coffin and Kraig stood on his tiptoes to look into the face of his beloved grandma. Everyone was silent. They, too wondered what this child would say and how he would handle the reality of death.

"Mama, may I touch her one more time?" he asked.

His hands rested on the pink satin of the coffin. I was hesitant. "Remember what I told you. She will be cold, not the warm grandma you are used to touching."

"I know," he said softly, "but I want to touch her just once more." And so I allowed him to reach in and touch his grandma's folded hands.

One brief touch. A precious look on his little face. Then he turned, looked at his grandma's many friends and family members and clearly announced, "That's not really my grandma, that's just her shell. My grandma is in heaven with Jesus."

I will never forget that moment. It was a lesson for every thoughtful person in that chapel. There were tears, but a little boy had made us think. Death is real, but so is heaven. Life at best here on earth is short, but heaven is forever.

I am helped by remembering A. W. Tozer's words:

> The days of the years of our lives are few, and swifter than a weaver's shuttle. Life is a short and fevered rehearsal for a concert we cannot stay to give. Just when we appear to have attained some proficiency we are forced to lay our instruments down.
>
> There is simply not time enough to think, to become, to perform what the constitution of our natures indicates we are capable of. How completely satisfying to turn from our limitations to a God who has none. Eternal years lie in His heart. For Him time does not pass, it remains; and those who are in Christ share with Him all the riches of limitless time and endless years . . . The gift of eternal life in Christ Jesus is as limitless as God.[1]

The Everlastingness of God and of Ourselves

"From everlasting to everlasting thou art God," Moses said. This concept of the everlastingness of God runs like a lofty mountain range throughout the Bible. As we let this thought permeate our thinking, life can take on new and deeper meaning as we prepare for our own everlastingness.

Classic literature echoes a theme that has always existed in the heart of mankind, an intense inner longing for immortality. We do not want to just die; we want to believe there is more. Tennyson, for instance, reasoned: "Thou wilt not leave us in the dust . . . Thou art just."

When it comes to life after death, faith in Jesus Christ is not optional. For it's either Christ or eternal tragedy. Paul's message resounds with hope for the thinking Christian woman, "Jesus Christ . . . has abolished death and brought life and immortality to light through the gospel" (2 Timothy 1:10).

As Christians we are pilgrims on the move, headed for a city whose builder and maker is God (Hebrews 11:10). Either we will arrive at our destination through the passageway of death, or we will be caught up in the rapture of the saints (1 Corinthians 15:51,52).

All people, however, Christian or not, will live forever. There are those who mistakenly believe the word "death" means nonexistence, that there is no such thing as a hereafter. But the Scriptures clearly show there is existence beyond the grave for all. How that existence will be spent depends on choices made while here on earth (Revelations 20:10-15). Both heaven *and* hell are realities we cannot ignore.

Our God is a God of love, but He is also a God of holiness and justice. He doesn't wink at sin; the unjust shall be punished (2 Peter 2:9). But He has provided a way of salvation. "For God so loved the world that He gave His only begotten Son, that *whoever believes in Him* should not perish but have everlasting life" (John 3:16).

It is our responsibility to share this Truth with people who are not committed to following Christ. This is not easy. Talking about hell doesn't win popularity contests.

Of course we don't grab people by the throats and say, "You're going to hell . . ." Rather, as opportunities present themselves, by our lives *and* by our words, we must speak the Truth with conviction born out of love and concern. As Martha Reapsome says in her book, *A Woman's Path to Godliness*, "It isn't either living a godly life before her *or* speaking about Jesus; it's both . . . No one can guess how to become a Christian just by watching a godly person."[2]

While I was writing this book, I had an opportunity to speak to a co-worker about the Lord one day. She brazenly admitted to being a non-believer, and was proud of her "smartness" in being able to detect falsity in the lives of many who professed to be Christians. Yet God gave me the words and an attitude that conveyed "I love you, I am concerned for your eternal destiny."

The Cost of the Journey

All we lose on our way to everlastingness is our old carnal nature and physical frame, the shell my young son so wisely recognized those long years ago as we stood by the coffin of my beloved mother. Kraig knew Grandma was gone, and he was right. Her spirit was with her heavenly Father. Because she had followed Christ, her name had been written in the Lamb's Book of Life. When she crossed through that passageway called "death," she was known and welcomed.

An Eternal Perspective on Material Possessions

While He was on earth, Jesus had quite a bit to say about dealing with material possessions. His comments on this issue appear in all four Gospels, including the account in Luke 12 in which He told the parable of the rich man who was concerned only with storing up riches on earth and had no interest in the things of God.

The focus of Christ's teachings on money and material possessions was not that there is inherent virtue in poverty and sin in riches. Rather, He plainly taught the greater value of heavenly treasure and the folly of spending all one's time and efforts on earthly pursuits. He gave stern warnings about the seductive power of riches or anything else that draws our hearts away from God and serving Him.

In his book, *The Golden Cow*, author John White elaborates on Christ's teachings. He points out that the rich young ruler was told to sell what he had and follow Jesus because he loved what he trusted, and he trusted his great possessions. He was a slave to the visible and lacked effective faith in the invisible God (Matthew 19:16-22). Christ didn't condemn him for possessing riches, only for hanging on to them above all else. He was enslaved by his wealth, and his values were askew.

There is undeniable peril in wealth when it is misused. As I look about me and see needs throughout the world as well as in my own community and church, I ache because God's people who are able to meet some of these needs are not doing it. Their giving is token, especially in contrast to what they have and keep for themselves. It is this attitude Jesus decried.

The degree of our concern for our neighbors (the world, the church, those we know who are without jobs, the homeless, the hungry, those who are struggling financially) shows itself in how we respond to their needs. This response, in turn, reflects our true relationship with God.

White says, "Riches corrupt everybody who is in the least corruptible. God is merciful and can deliver the rich from the danger of being rich. But many of us do not want to be delivered. We say we trust God. But we act as though our trust is in riches as indeed it often is. Riches undermine faith."[3]

Eternal Values in All Things

Whether it concerns her own or others' lives, the thinking Christian woman *knows* her thoughts, words and actions have eternal consequences. It is that knowledge that motivates her to evaluate *all* areas of her life in light of God's eternal values rather than the temporal ones of this world.

She is careful to ask, "Would God approve of this (action, attitude, etc.)? Does it compare well with what the Bible teaches? Does this match with the character of God I see revealed in the life of Christ?" Seeing God's values alongside ours or those of our society raises a standard that provides an important safeguard as we make both the big and little choices of our lives.

Think on These Things ...

Principle: Because the thinking Christian woman has a well-defined value system, she lives with eternity's values in view. Jesus said, "Watch therefore, for you do not know what hour your Lord is coming" (Matthew 24:42).

God's Word says, "Live life, then, with a due sense of responsibility, not as [wo]men who do not know the meaning of life but as those who do. Make the best use of your time, despite all the evils of these days" (Ephesians 5:15,16, Phillips).

1. When you think of eternity, what thoughts come to mind?
2. Write down some hindrances to your living with eternity's values in view.
3. Define your values. Are they the best, in keeping with such passages as these: Matthew 6:19-24;

19:16-30 (also Luke 18:18-30); Luke 9:23 (also Mark 10:38); Luke 12:13-34; 14:25-33; 16:19-31?
4. How can we apply the passages listed in number 3 in today's culture?

She Is Disciplined; She Values and Guards Her Time

So don't be anxious about tomorrow. God will take care of your tomorrow too. Live one day at time.
(Matthew 6:34, TLB)

The old cliché, "Man works from sun to sun, but a woman's work is never done," rings true for many of us. It doesn't seem to matter if you are a full-time homemaker or a career woman. Women tell me they never seem to have enough time to do all the things they want to do. Time is always at a premium.

———————————— ❋ ————————————

Principle

The thinking Christian woman is disciplined, values and guards her time and sets priorities.

———————————— ❋ ————————————

Many years ago while my children were still small and I found myself frustrated because there never seemed to be enough hours in the day, I came to a glaring realization: I needed to learn to properly value time. Several factors brought this conclusion into focus, not the least of which was admitting that if God intended for us to have 40-hour days, He'd have made them that way. Complaining wouldn't change the fact that in the course of an average day I had about 16 hours to accomplish what was needed. Time was God's gift, worthy of *careful investment*.

About that time I saw a piece of pop art that grabbed my attention. It depicted a melted plastic alarm clock with the caption: TIME MELTS AWAY.

Not long afterwards my daughter came to me with beads of perspiration glistening on her forehead. It was an extremely warm day and she'd been playing hard. In a frightened voice she exclaimed, "Oh mother, I'm melting!"

The conjunction of those happenings gripped my thinking. Sometimes we do have the feeling that time is melting away and so are we. We ask, "Where does the time go?" or we make excuses, "When I have more time..."

I already knew the world was full of disorganized people who had lost control of their time. That day I determined that I wouldn't be one of them.

Searching for Solutions

That determination prompted me to begin an important search. What did the Bible and different writers have to say about time? How could I maximize my time? In the brief period Jesus lived on this earth He somehow managed to command His time in an extraordinary fashion. How did He do that?

I clearly saw that I needed to define priorities and goals (both short-term and long-term). I needed to determine what was robbing me of time, how I might be losing or wasting it and what God expected from me in the use of it.

I was a mother of three small children at that time, as well as being involved in our family business. (Later another son completed our family.) Further, God had given me the ability to write, and had provided opportunities for me to exercise that ability.

I wanted to be a good steward, but there were a lot of demands on my time. I was determined not to short-change my family, for I knew that would be a defiant, disobedient response to God's goodness. I decided to *seek* His help in sorting it all out.

I recently found these notes in one of my journal entries—a reminder to me now that I was serious about pursuing this subject:

> I need a definition of time. *Time*: A precious gift of God. A period of opportunity and grace which God wants me to use wisely, fulfilling His purpose for my life. Truly one of the most valuable possessions I have.

That may not be the best definition in the world, but it met my need. In that same journal, I found these notes:

> Thomas Edison said: "Time is the most valuable thing in the world."
> John Bunyan said: "He who runs from God in the morning will scarcely find Him the rest of the day."
> Thomas Carlyle wrote: "It is one of the illusions that the present hour is not the critical decisive hour. Write it on your heart that every day is the best day of the year."

There were other journal entries, but the important point is that I had begun a search that would yield dividends for the rest of my life. I'd become familiar with the old equation, "Time is money." Since most of us don't have enough of either, I was determined to conserve both.

It was the Word of God, however, that really defined the value of time for me. In the apostle Paul's letters I heard him say, "Value your time; make the most of it" (Ephesians 5:16). In Corinthians I read, ". . . brethren, the time is short" (1 Corinthians 7:29).

Jesus' discourse on worry in Matthew 6 provided powerful impetus to live one day at a time. The more I studied His life and ministry, the more I saw how unhurried His pace was, and yet amazingly, how much was accomplished. As I focused on Jesus' life, I saw that He understood His own limits.

Jesus limited? Yes. He was fully man even though He was God in the flesh. Because of this, He lived within the confines of time as we know it. Yet Jesus didn't live frantically, feverishly running from one demanding situation into another. He didn't let others dictate His responses to human need. He wasn't trying to impress anyone.

Ministering to people was His highest priority. He came to teach, preach and serve, and His ultimate purpose was to die. He always responded to demands made upon His time in light of those priorities.

Jesus never had to play catch-up. He was never caught short on time. He was flexible, which is important and can be seen as you observe His life as recorded in the Gospels. Jesus had His priorities in order because He properly valued time. Further, Jesus always took time to pray, to be alone with His thoughts with the Father. Before every decision and action, before every word spoken, He needed heavenly insights for earthly tasks. If He, how much more do we!

No one wants to be reminded that his or her time of life on earth is short and, at best, uncertain. The psalmist speaks of the average life span as being "threescore years and ten" (Psalm 90:10). Although he adds that if you are strong, you might add another 10 years as sort of a bonus for right living, still "we spend our years as a tale that is told" (v. 9, KJV).

I made a covenant with God during those searching years long ago. I wrote:

> Stewardship is the measure of a person's love—the package in which he gives himself to You. Father, help me to be a good steward and to always value time.

Andrew Murray wrote: "God is ready to assume full responsibility for the life wholly yielded to Him."

That's reassuring. But how do we do it? With so many demands on us as women, how do we structure our lives so that yieldedness to Him is as natural as breathing? It requires a decision of our will.

In my journal I wrote:

> Since time is such a special gift, it is not to be squandered, on the other hand neither is it to be hoarded just for my own selfish ends; but it is to be invested, wisely, in enjoyable and satisfying pursuits, in needful ways for the greatest possible good of my family, others, and for myself.

Psychiatrist Rollo May says, "Will is the capacity to organize one's self so that movement in a certain direction or toward a certain goal may take place." Important words. It implies the need for discipline.

A New Definition for Discipline

As I worked through the issue of properly valuing time, I wrote a definition for discipline that seemed to fit my thinking:

> Doing what you must do while resisting what you want to do, *but* keeping in mind what you really want, and then working to bring about the fulfillment of your dreams and aspirations with God's help and in His time.

The thinking Christian woman defines her needs, goals and desires, but recognizes her desires are not always needful, although they can be rewarding and pleasing. She acknowledges that to meet her needs and gratify some of her desires, she has to press on to accomplish her goals. The thinking Christian woman recognizes the road to accomplishment is paved with more than a *"want to,"* but a willingness *"to do."*

Years ago at the outset of my writing career, I attended a conference where Ethel Barrett, the prolific writer, spoke. She radiated enthusiasm, and I asked God to let it rub off on me. Instead, He directed me to Colossians 3:23 and 24—verses that became my "writing verses" and have motivated me now all these years, "And whatsoever ye do, do it heartily, as to the Lord, and not unto men, knowing that from the Lord you will receive the reward . . . for you serve the Lord Christ."

Three words stood out clearly: DO IT HEARTILY. The message was obvious. Just because I'd had a meaningful experience in which I felt God was telling me He could use my love of writing, it did not mean it would happen automatically. He expected effort from me. My ability to write was necessary, but my availability was more important to Him. He needed my willingness *to do* something. Also, God was telling me how to do it: "Heartily," with enthusiasm. J. B. Phillips translates that, "Put your whole heart and soul into it."

Everyone, it seems, has a book in them. People are always coming up to me and saying, "Oh, I want to write a book . . ." If I were to see these same people a year from now, they'd probably say the same thing. People want to *have written*, but they don't want to *write*. They want to play the piano, but they don't want to invest the time in learning how. They want to do any number of things, but they do not discipline themselves to achieve them.

With discipline, one has a handle on life. Without it, one is constantly burning one's hand on the pot. With discipline, you have a means for reaching from wish to fulfillment. Without discipline, you can only stare like a windowshopper at the things you want from life.

The Gracious "No"

Discipline has simplified my life. It has made me recognize the need to be a decision-maker and eliminate procrastination. And it has taught me the art of graciously saying "No" when necessary. Years ago when my first book was published, a friend came up to me at an autographing, put her arms around me and said, "Now I know why you've had to say *no* so often."

Discipline is not primarily external; it is internal. It's gentle, not punitive. It's worth cultivating. The rewards are fantastic. Today, as a result of learning this discipline, I can look back on productive years—years of doing what I could with the gifts God entrusted to me. There were times, I'm sure, when people did not understand. They may not understand you either at times. But remember that God has called us, and we are responsible to Him.

Christ provides the perfect example of disciplined use of time and of graciously saying "No" when needed. He moved with such freedom from the pressures others tried to bring to bear upon him (John 4:31-34). He didn't succumb to the demands of those who would like to have dictated His course of action. Even His own mother couldn't distract Him from what He had set out to do (John 2:3,4).

Jesus wasn't primarily concerned with what others thought. Their opinions weren't the criteria by which He made His decisions. Rather, Jesus knew who He was in His Father's eyes and that's what really mattered. First and foremost, He was responsible to the Father. Because time is so valuable, "the coin of your life," as Carl Sandburg once said, we have to guard it lest others spend it for us.

Time is the very essence of life. As such it always will seem in short supply. The ultimate realization of what is God's best for you and your family, as well as the fulfillment of your goals, dreams and desires, depends upon proper use of time. That's why it's vital that we cultivate the discipline to resist what author Charles Hummel calls the "tyranny of the urgent," the all too prevalent tendency to immediately respond to the people and things in our lives that simply cry the loudest for attention.

Effort is the ore from which satisfaction is mined, but it happens in the context of the wise use of time. God wants you to be the master of the time He has allotted to you, not its slave. He has sown seeds of potential within your being and wants to see you fulfilled. Discipline is the key to wise stewardship of the gifts and time He has given us.

---- ----

Principle

Seek ways to enhance the quality of your time. Efficient management of one's time is something that can be learned and developed.

---- ----

Busy doesn't necessarily mean productive. In addition to those areas already discussed, here are some other practical ideas that can help reduce the tensions and frustrations that result from being disorganized.

1. Work smarter not harder. That may mean investing some time to make time. Do it. Plan. Schedule. Goals can be personal statements of faith. Carefully think through your own situation. Are there habits/patterns of disorganization that need to be broken? Resolve to seize control of your time.

2. Write things down. Don't push your memory too hard. Beware of the possibility of overload. Thoughts can be fleeting; capture them. Unclutter your thinking. Use a "Things to do list."

3. Plan ahead. Avoid stress and possible errors in judgment that can result when pressure leads to hasty decisions. Victor Hugo wrote, "When the disposal of time is surrendered to the chance of incidents, chaos will result." If you fail to plan, you plan to fail.

4. Be flexible. Don't get uptight or feel like a failure if your best laid plans go awry. It happens. Learn to bend. Schedules and plans are not ends in themselves; whatever helps you function at your best is what you are after. That's what flexibility is all about.

5. Learn to make decisions; kick the procrastination habit. Because procrastination is psychological, it can

be quite draining. Try to understand why you delay making decisions. Are you afraid of failing, making a mistake, rejection? Do you fear offending someone? Thinking through your reasons can help you avoid the paralysis of procrastination. Isolate the why and move on from there. Seek God's perspective in your decision-making and trust Him. If you've made a wrong decision, it's not the end of the road. Get up and go on.

6. Develop a sense of your mission in life. What has God called you to do? What is the best possible use of your time? Seek to rule out the non-essentials. Determine what the non-negotiables are.

--- ---

Principle

The thinking Christian woman knows her relationship with God comes first . . . before anything else. Matthew 6:33 is real to her. "But seek first the kingdom of God . . ." She knows she needs God's perspective in every area of her life.

--- ---

The thinking Christian woman has a well-defined value system that can stand up under the scrutiny of the Father. If we could see ourselves through His eyes, we would stand amazed at the vast untapped potential.

Also, the thinking Christian woman recognizes that to everything there is a season. Solomon understood this principle. He talked about it in Ecclesiastes 3. "There is a right time for everything" (v. 1, TLB).

The apostle Paul understood this principle as well. He wrote, "I am still not all I should be but I am bringing all my energies to bear on this one thing: Forgetting the past and looking forward to what lies ahead, I strain to reach the prize for which God is calling us up to heaven because of what Christ Jesus did for us" (Philippians 3:13,14, TLB). At the end of his life, Paul was able to write, "I have fought the good fight, I have finished the race, I have kept the faith" (2 Timothy 4:7).

Poet Horatius Bonar challenges my thinking with these words:

> Fill up the hours with what will last;
> Buy up the moments as they go.
> The life above, when this is past,
> Is the ripe fruit of life below.

The psalmist knew the limits of his time and the value of living that time in harmony with God's will:

> Lord, help me to realize how brief my time
> on earth will be. Help me to know that I am
> here for but a moment more. My life is no
> longer than my hand! My whole lifetime is but
> a moment to you ... And so, Lord, my only
> hope is in you (Psalm 39:4,5,7, TLB).

Think on These Things ...

Principle: The thinking Christian woman is disciplined, values and guards her time and sets priorities and goals. She seeks ways to enhance the quality of her time, and recognizes that to everything there is a season.

God's Word says, "But seek first the kingdom of God and His righteousness, and all these things will be added to you. So don't be anxious about tomorrow. God will take care of your tomorrow too. Live one day at a time" (Matthew 6:33,34, TLB).

1. How much time have you consciously or unconsciously wasted today?
2. How much additional time could have been yours if you had planned the day and thought things through?
3. Was your attention and participation absolutely required in a particular meeting or situation?
4. What goal could you have achieved if you had organized your time, set priorities and plotted your course?
5. What does living one day at a time mean to you? Are you satisfied with the way your time is spent? If not, what can and will you do about it?

Part IV

The Thinking Christian Woman Nurtures Her Relationships

Your body is the flesh that clothes His Presence.
—Anne Ortlund[1]

In a world like ours there is and always will be plenty of important work for the thoughtful, reverent [wo]man to do. Morally the world is like a bombed city. The streets are blocked, the buildings lie in ruins and the wounded and homeless wait for the healing services of men and women who can help them in their distress.
—A. W. Tozer[2]

Therefore, as God's chosen people, holy and dearly loved, clothe yourselves with compassion, kindness, humility, gentleness and patience. Bear with each other and forgive whatever grievances you may have against one another. Forgive as the Lord forgave you. And over all these virtues put on love, which binds them all together in perfect unity.
—Colossians 3:12-14 NIV

She Communicates and Saturates
Her Relationships with Love 🔥

Love never fails.
(1 Corinthians 13:8)

While traveling in Europe gathering material for a book, I saw a motto on the desk of the director of Trans-World Radio in Monte Carlo, Monaco, that attracted my attention. It read, *Communication is a painfully troublesome thing—it takes a lot of love.*

"Troublesome"? That made me think. It seemed so negative. I didn't dispute the truth of the statement, but surely there was a more positive way to say it. Then it dawned on me.

Following my mother's death, a friend of hers told me, "Helen, mothers are the glue that holds families together in many instances. Your mother certainly did that. It's going to take a lot of effort on the part of someone to keep your family in touch with each other. Will you be that someone? It will take communication and love."

Yes, I had connected with the motto. No wonder I identified with it. I had discovered that what this woman had shared with me was undeniably true.

Love cannot afford to be anything but lavish. Even extravagant. Yet it has nothing to do with money. Dollars-and-cents value is not the measure by which love is to be evaluated. In the final analysis, it costs nothing to lavishly give love. It can, however, cost everything. A paradox. We can say we love, but we prove it when we back up our words with action.

Principle

The thinking Christian woman communicates and saturates her relationships with love.

Several years ago, a popular song capitalized on these words, "Love makes the world go 'round, love makes the world go 'round." I don't think anyone would deny that this is what it takes—a lot of loving in your own little world to touch the great big world.

It's difficult to adequately describe love, but one thing is certain. Genuine love is not passive. It's always active. When you love someone you are happiest when you are *doing* something for them, *helping* them in some way, *sharing* with them, *giving* them something. *Love seeks ways to express itself.*

Nurturing Family Relationships

When my children were little, I read something that significantly colored my thinking. William Wordsworth wrote words to this effect: "The best portion of a good man's life consists of little, nameless acts of kindness and love. Little things do mean a lot."

At the time I thought to myself, *Helen, you are building a storehouse of memories for your children in the "dailyness" of being a mother. Do a good job while you have the opportunity.*

Someone once told me, "Let childhood happen." It distresses me to see parents rushing their children through those precious years, not savoring the moments. The path to happiness for our children involves our patiently loving and helping them all along the way, from infancy through young adulthood. Ideally, it should be done without hurry. We need to give them time to be children.

Now many years later as I see my adult children struggling through trying times in parenting their little ones, I'm glad I invested as much love as I did in them. How gratifying it is to listen in on their conversation and hear them reminiscing, "Remember when..."

The thinking Christian woman is devoted to her family. She looks well to the ways of her household (Proverbs 31:27). The description of a worthy woman as outlined in this Proverbs passage portrays an industrious lady who excels in many ways. She's energetic and hard working. "Her children arise and call her blessed, her husband also, and he praises her: Many women do noble things, but you surpass them all" (vv. 28,29, NIV). Obviously, this kind of woman saturates her relationships with love—unconditional love.

In the course of writing a book on parenting adult children, I sent out 500 questionnaires and interviewed many husbands and wives. As I tallied responses and comments, the consensus was clear. Parenting demands unconditional love. This doesn't mean we necessarily approve of everything going on in the lives of our adult children, but it does mean we still love them and convey that to them.

When our children are little they step on our toes; when they are big they step on our hearts. And that can be a heavy tread. But regardless of the heartaches and disappointments they may bring into their lives and ours, parents need to keep loving their children, never giving up hope.

Love and Marriage

"A worthy wife is her husband's joy and crown; the other kind corrodes his strength and tears down everything he does" (Proverbs 12:4, TLB).

Relationships are no stronger than the commitment we make to them, and this is especially true in marriage. Society as we know it today is very unsupportive of long-term commitments, especially when they require sacrifice. Commitment, however, is the mortar of relationships. Without it relationships don't last, nor do they meet the needs of others.

Women are generally "givers" by nature. Biologically it began this way, and this quality continues on and manifests itself, for instance, in the sensitive relationships between mother and child. Women excel in loving because we have to be self-sacrificing, unselfish and understanding if good relationships are to flourish in our homes.

When our relationships are not all we desire them to be, it is wise to turn our thoughts to Jesus. This is not simplistic advice. Christ, our example, made an irreversible commitment to us. Consider His life—the ridicule, rejection, scorn and suffering. When you think you can't forgive any more, when you're weary of being trampled on, when your relationships are ruptured and rotten even though you've tried so hard, fix your thoughts on Jesus. Fixing our minds on His example allows us to experience peace through the storms. By focusing on Him we can have a serenity, stability and security that will enable us to saturate our relationships with love even when all around us is anything but lovely.

As we cultivate the kind of love described in 1 Corinthians 13, we help our husbands, families and ourselves build a storehouse of precious memories. This is Christian love at its highest and best. It embraces many virtues, all giving evidence of deep caring.

The Way of Love

As I thought about the many words I could write about love, I was overwhelmed because so much has already been written. Then I realized there was no way I could improve on the apostle Paul's summary in 1 Corinthians 13. I am partial to the Phillips translation:

> If I speak with the eloquence of men and of angels, but have no love, I become no more than blaring brass or crashing cymbal. If I have the gift of foretelling the future and hold in my hand not only all human knowledge but the very secrets of God, and if I have that absolute faith which can remove mountains, but have no love, I amount to nothing at all. If I dispose my own body to be burned, but have no love, I achieve precisely nothing. This love of which I speak is slow to lose patience—it looks for a way of being constructive. It is not possessive: it is neither anxious to impress nor does it cherish inflated ideas of its own importance.
>
> Love has good manners and does not pursue selfish advantage. It is not touchy. It does not keep account of evil or gloat over the wickedness of other people. On the contrary, it shares the joy of those who live by the truth.
>
> Love knows no limit to its endurance, no end to

its trust, no fading of its hope; it can outlast anything. Love never fails.

In this life we have three lasting qualities—faith, hope and love. But the greatest of them is love (vv. 1-8a,13).

Paul's letter to the Colossian Christians contains guidelines for holy living, based on the kind of love described above. He said, "Most of all, let love guide your life, for then the whole church will stay together in perfect harmony" (Colossians 3:14, NIV).

This instruction also applies to us as individuals for we have to live with ourselves. Years ago I taught my children a little maxim which hangs in the halls of my mind, *I have to live with myself and so, I want to be fit for myself to know.* To be fit for myself to know, I have to live in the way of love.

In Romans 13, Paul said the most important command of our Lord was to love one another (vv. 8-10). This is the fulfillment of the law, the law of love. "None of us lives to himself," Paul explained. "Conduct yourself by the standard of love" (Romans 14:7,15, AMP). "So let us then definitely aim for and eagerly pursue what makes for harmony and for mutual upbuilding of one another" (v. 19, AMP).

However, we aren't perfect saints; sometimes we stumble along the way of love. There are times when our humanness gets in the way of maintaining our relationships. But if we admit our humanness and fallibility and say to those we love, "I'm sorry, I haven't been as loving [patient, kind, thoughtful, understanding . . .] as I should be . . ." we can pave the way for love to function again as the Father desires. This is love communicating. And *it can be painfully troublesome.*

The Outworking of Love

The thinking Christian woman consciously works to develop her strengths and strengthen her weaknesses. This may mean admitting she isn't always right.

One day author Keith Miller sat across from me in a restaurant in Whittier, California, and said, "The freedom to be one's self is better than carrying the burden of trying to be perfect." I needed to hear that. I was going through a period of time when I felt I'd let my children, my friends, our church and the Lord down. I was carrying a heavy load of guilt and sadness. Keith helped me see it was okay to admit my weaknesses. My relationships began to improve after that.

Jesus knows not only the wickedness of sinners, but the weaknesses of saints. And so do those with whom we live and work. Love doesn't demand that we be perfect. However, it does ask us to try.

In our relationships, we need to do what is necessary to be love personified. Christ is Christianity's greatest credential; we should seek to reflect His image. Jesus' life demonstrates love in action, and gives us an ideal to work toward. He cares all the time—even when we're imperfect and fall far short of the ideal. If we say we care about others, our goal should be to follow Christ's example.

My caring tells others I am affected by their triumphs and their trials. I hope for the same kind of loving care from them, yet I know from past hurtful experiences that is not always the case. Sometimes even those we love most let us down. They don't always empathize with us; they don't always even try.

However, when others disappoint us or vice versa, it is not always intentional. Sometimes we are too busy, preoccupied with our own plans and problems. Sometimes we are just plain tired. There's simply not enough emotional energy left at day's end to write the letters, make the phone calls or do what is necessary to nurture our relationships.

One cannot and must not place her reliance on people alone. We need to teach this truth to our children when they are small, and remind our adult children as well. Moreover, we need to remind ourselves. Let us not be hasty in judging the motives of others, or ascribe certain behavior to them. We do not always know all the circumstances. We haven't "walked in their moccasins."

One of my daughters has had to work through some stormy times in her marriage (her story is related in my book, *You Never Stop Being a Parent*). On many occasions she has called to say, "Thank you, Mom, for teaching us about how to respond with love. It really works. Hard, yes, but so necessary."

The Imperative of Love

So often we pray, "Dear God, give me more of Your love so I can show it to others." He *is* love (1 John 4:16). Our part is to permit love to become a habit by practicing it in our human relationships.

We begin by beginning. For some, loving comes easily; for others it is more difficult. Not that they are necessarily unloving, but their natures are more restrained. However, all of us love through the power of the Holy Spirit living in us. John, best known as "the apostle of love," reminds us we should love one another and in so doing reveal whether we are a true child of God.

"Little children," he wrote, "let us stop just saying we love people, let us really love them, and show it by our actions. Then we will know for sure, by our actions, that we are on God's side, and our consciences will be clear, even when we stand before the Lord . . . And this is what God says we must do: Believe on the name of his Son Jesus Christ, and love one another. Those who do what God says—they are living with God and He with them. We know this is true because the Holy Spirit He has given us tells us so" (1 John 3:18,19,23,24b, TLB).

When one of my children was little he asked me, "Mommy, how can God love everybody. Is He magic?"

He was genuinely perplexed. How could God possibly love everybody, when there are so many of us? To a child's way of thinking, it would take nothing short of magic!

Jesus Gives a New Commandment

But you and I know God is much more than magic. In John 13 we see Jesus giving His disciples a new commandment, "Dear, dear children, how brief are these moments before I must go away and leave you! Then, though you search for Me, you cannot come to Me . . . And so I am giving a new commandment to you now— love each other just as much as I love you. Your strong love for each other will prove to the world that you are My disciples" (John 13:33-35, TLB).

Jesus knew how unlovable people were (and are). He knew how unappreciative, unkind, thoughtless, selfish, quick to judge and criticize, and how very mean human nature can be. Even within that intimate circle of 12 there was envy, disputing and dissension. And these were the men Jesus was counting on to spread the Gospel! So it was that Jesus, just hours before His crucifixion, gave this diverse group the supreme command, "Love one another."

How were they to do that? How are *we* to love one another?

The Old Testament Commandment said they were to love the Lord with all their heart, soul, strength and mind, and their neighbor as they loved themselves (Luke 10:27-37). The New Commandment instructed them to love as Jesus loved.

How did Jesus love? First, "He loved them to the last and to the highest degree" (John 13:1, AMP). He loved them to the end, to the fullest extent. Jesus loved with everything He had.

Second, He loved with the heart of a servant—He washed their feet (vv. 4,5). The towel Jesus wore about His waist as He served them was in that culture a badge of slavery. What humility. John never forgot it; neither did Peter. "Gird yourselves with humility," he wrote decades afterward as he remembered it all (1 Peter 5:5). Would you have gotten just a bit squeamish at the thought of washing 12 pairs of dirty feet at mealtime? But Christ did it! He who was equal with God rose from the table, laid aside His glory and took the form of a servant, thereby demonstrating an important aspect of love. If we are to communicate and saturate our relationships with love, it will be through loving as Jesus loved. It will mean doing whatever we can to ensure the happiness and well-being of others, lessening their heartaches and multiplying their joys.

Third, Jesus showed us what love is all about in His unconditional response to carrying out the Father's will. He loved us to death—His own death. He laid down His life for us. "No one has greater love . . . than to lay down his own life for his friends" (John 15:13, AMP). The apostle Paul spoke of Christ's love by saying He loved the church and gave Himself up for her (Ephesians 5:25). [Paul used this phrase by way of analogy, calling husbands to love their wives in this way. Think what would happen to the divorce rate across the nation if this kind of love were genuinely practiced.]

What an extreme commitment is involved when an individual reaches the point where he is willing to love as Jesus loved. Would the disciples pass the test?

History proves they did. The Christian Church that has come down to us through the centuries is a living testimony to the fact that the disciples excelled in brotherly love. And not only they, but many others caught the spirit they demonstrated and the early Church flourished and grew. The Word of God and Christ's love spread dynamically through those 11 remarkable men. Historians speak of the glory of the early Church in terms of the love they demonstrated for one another and even those outside the Church.

Love runs as a constant theme throughout the New Testament. Nothing is emphasized as much as the love that seeks to show the love of Jesus. Even adversaries of the early Christians took notice of this love, exclaiming, "See how those Christians love one another!"

One of the hallmarks of the thinking Christian woman's life is the love she continually pours out on others. Let this, then, be the aim of our lives, the prayer on our lips and the motivating force in our individual experience... that all people shall know that we, too, are Christ's disciples because we have love for one another.

Think on These Things...

Principle: The thinking Christian woman nurtures her relationships. She communicates and saturates her relationships with love. Love is the distinguishing characteristic of her life.

God's Word says, "Love never fails" (1 Corinthians 13:8).

One of my favorite writers is Amy Carmichael. In her devotional titled *If* she wrote:

> Beloved, let us love.
> Lord, what is love?
> Love is that which inspired My life, and led
> Me to My Cross, and held Me on My cross.
> Love is that which will make it thy joy to lay
> down thy life for thy brethren.
> Lord, evermore give me that love.
> "Blessed are they which do hunger and
> thirst after love, for they shall be filled."[1]

1. On a scale of 1 to 10, with 10 being the highest, rate yourself on the love scale below:

Love	I am	Action I Will Take
is patient		
is kind		
does not envy		
does not boast		
is not rude		
is not self-seeking		
is not easily angered		
keeps no record of wrongs		
does not delight in evil		
rejoices in truth		
always protects		

always trusts
always hopes
always perseveres
never fails

2. Read 1 John chapters 3 and 4. Write out your understanding and response.

3. Here are 13 ways the New Testament tells us to communicate with each other as Christians:

    1. Suffering together: 1 Corinthians 12:26.
    2. Rejoicing together: Romans 12:15.
    3. Carrying one another's burdens: Galatians 6:2.
    4. Restoring one another: Galatians 6:1.
    5. Praying for one another: Romans 15:30.
    6. Teaching and admonishing one another: Colossians 3:16.
    7. Refreshing one another: Romans 15:32.
    8. Encouraging one another: Romans 1:12.
    9. Forgiving one another: Ephesians 4:32.
    10. Confessing to one another: James 5:16.
    11. Being truthful with one another: Ephesians 4:25.
    12. Spurring one another toward good deeds: Hebrews 10:24.
    13. Giving to one another: Philippians 4:14, 15.

On a scale of 1 to 10, with 10 being the highest, rate yourself on your communication and relationships. Another word for all of the above is what?

She Is an Encourager; She Is Considerate and Seeks to Bring Out the Best in Others 🎵

> One of the highest of human duties is the duty of encouragement. It is easy to laugh at men's ideals; it is easy to pour cold water on their enthusiasm; it is easy to discourage others. The world is full of discouragers. We have a Christian duty to encourage one another. Many a time a word of praise or thanks or appreciation or cheer has kept a man on his feet. Blessed is the man who speaks such a word.[1]
> (William Barclay)

"If you have any encouragement from being united with Christ, if any comfort from His love, if any fellowship with the Spirit, if any tenderness and compassion, then make my joy complete by being like-minded, having the same love, being one in spirit and purpose" (Philippians 2:1, NIV).

Ah, what refreshing words those are. Just to read them is to feel affirmed, and how much we all need that. I have yet to meet a man, woman, young person or child who doesn't need encouragement.

A pat on the back is so much better than a kick in the rear. That doesn't sound very ladylike, but there are times when I'm not as ladylike as I should be and I've said those very words. If you've experienced any of those kicks when you've been down, then you know what I'm talking about.

Remember that old song Gene Autrey used to sing, "Oh give me a home, where the buffalo roam, and the deer and the antelope play. Where seldom is heard, a discouraging word..." In our society, "discouraging words" are frequently heard. We search in vain for that "encouraging word" as we mingle with the masses in our overly populated world, obsessed with identity-crisis experiences, networking, latchkeying, climbing for the upper regions of career success and striving for excellence.

--- ---

Principle

The thinking Christian woman is an encourager. She seeks to bring out the best in others; she is a giver offering help and hope. She is considerate.

--- ---

Today possibly more than ever we need what the apostle Paul talked about in his Philippian letter as he emphasized encouraging one another, "Is there any such thing as Christians cheering each other up? Do you love me enough to want to help me? Does it mean anything to you that we are brothers in the Lord, sharing the same Spirit? Are your hearts tender and sympathetic at all? Then make me truly happy by loving each other, working together with one heart and mind and purpose. Don't be selfish...Be humble, thinking of others... Don't just think about your own affairs, but be interested in others, too, and in what they are doing" (Philippians 2:1-4, TLB).

Upon reflection, most of us can probably recollect some events in our lives that were pretty heavy in tipping us off balance. Others were less earthshaking. Perhaps you've even experienced a "winter of discontent," when you wondered if the effort of living was worth it.

In my research and writing, I have discovered that almost everyone has wished for an out on occasion. Statistics show 90 percent of the population has contemplated suicide at one time or another. Ask 10 different people whether they have considered it, and the very reticence of some to reply provides the clue that they have.

It is not uncommon for people to experience, one or more times in their lives, a deep immobilizing despair that saps creative energy and drive. With it often comes loss of the will to live. There is an eclipse in the soul.

Many things can trigger discouraging moments— rotten or ruptured relationships, lack of financial resources, on-the-job stress, loneliness, alienation or isolation from others, scholastic anxiety, poor health, feelings of failure.

And failure can wear a thousand faces. It is no respecter of persons and stalks many an unsuspecting victim. The result of any of these circumstances can be a bankruptcy of spirit, the consequences of which, if left unattended, can be devastating.

Yet longing for death or contemplating suicide is not the ultimate "geographic cure." While we can't deny that in dying a person changes his or her location from earth to someplace else, it is far better to seek God's solution for one's dilemmas. What is missing? *Hope.* Encouragement.

A suicide attempt is a cry for help. And a cry for help is a summons to rescue. Will you be that someone who offers help and hope?

I remember the painful days following my divorce—the sense of aloneness, being cut off from understanding others. I recall walking down the grocery store aisle, seeing a friend coming my way, feeling suddenly encouraged and hopeful and then watching her turn her cart and go the other direction when she saw me. My stock in the reliability of Christian friends plummeted to the bottom. That "kick in the rear" was extremely hurtful.

It is important to remember at the low tides in our lives, when it appears our Christian friends have forgotten us, that we are not to judge Christ by the neglect and failure of those who name His name but do not walk as He walked.

We must also consider that sometimes the "important others" in our lives simply do not recognize our needs. I learned that when we experienced a crisis with one of my sons and his family. I am grateful that Rosie, one of the women in our church, had the courage to remind me that sometimes we have to swallow our pride and let our needs be known. As a result of that experience, we, our son and his children were helped tremendously and were greatly encouraged in the Lord. (His wife had been institutionalized for a mental health problem).

Walking Love

Henry Drummond made this observation, "How many prodigals are kept out of the kingdom of God by the unlovely characters of those who profess to be inside!"

That is an indictment I never want to be guilty of, and I imagine you feel the same way. We are to be "walking love." We can be hope with shoes on, help with hands that are willing to give a needed pat on the back or friendly hugs.

Practice dispensing a smile and a word of encouragement on your daily rounds—in the market, at the restaurant, to a co-worker, to your child, to your husband. It takes so little to warm another's heart.

"You look very pretty today." *Think* of what that remark could mean to the waitress who is running her legs off to keep customers happy. Look for ways to give someone a reason to go on. The thinking Christian woman is an encourager.

A Commitment to Encouragement

In the New Testament we find a character whose name actually meant "Son of Encouragement." The introduction to Barnabas comes in Acts 4:36. It's such a short reference that it's easily overlooked. Yet here is a wonderful wise Christian man who came to the rescue of the early Church in a marvelously benevolent way. Author/ teacher Chuck Swindoll points out that in comparison to some of the other shining lights of the book of Acts— Peter, Paul, Silas, James and Apollos—Barnabas appears as a flickering flame. But never underestimate the influence of the Barnabases in the church!

The young, persecuted assembly of Christians at Jerusalem was under attack and desperately in need of encouragement. One of their big problems was finances. Along comes this Son of Encouragement from the island of Cyprus. Hearing of the believers' situation, he sold a tract of land and brought the money to the apostles for distribution to those in need. Swindoll calls this "encouragement in finances."

As a result of this kind act, the "good news" begins spreading like fire. It's too big for the leaders to handle. They need help—gifted assistance.

Enter Barnabas with Saul of Tarsus (Acts 11:25). Because of his notorious reputation for persecuting the Christians before his dramatic encounter with Jesus on the Damascus Road (Acts 9), Saul was still suspect in the eyes of many. But Barnabas goes to bat for Saul. Before the entire assembly, the "Son of Encouragement" pushes Saul into the limelight. From that point on, the spotlight focuses on Paul's ministry (and there is a name change). "Barney the Preacher" falls into second place.

It takes a great man or woman of God to give recognition where it is due—to be an encourager and step aside when someone else's God-given abilities are being used, and then to give that person one's full support. Swindoll calls this the "encouragement of fellowship and followship."

Sadly, this humble attitude is lacking in many churches today. The "green uglies" often get in the way—jealousy and its bitter fruit—and can be so damaging to the movement of the Holy Spirit in the church. This can also happen at one's job, or among one's children or friends.

Recorded in Acts 15 is one other noteworthy way Barnabas demonstrated encouragement. Paul and Barnabas' second missionary journey is about to begin, and they are discussing the possibility of taking John Mark along. Earlier, this young man had chosen not to take part in the rigors of the first missionary journey (Acts 13:13). The discussion became rather heated. Paul said John Mark couldn't go along, that he'd failed once and he'd fail again. Barnabas admitted this was true, but added, "We need to give him another chance; all he needs is a little encouragement."

The outcome? Paul sailed off with Silas; Barnabas went another direction with John Mark. *Encouragers demonstrate encouragement in spite of past failure.*

We need to ask ourselves, "Are we withholding encouragement from someone who has let us down in the past? Is there someone who would benefit from a loving demonstration of encouragement from us? We need to give that encouragement, doing it as unto the Lord. Such is the essential posture so desperately needed in our world today—the willingness to forgive and forget the past, to move on into the present offering help, hope and encouragement.

The Encourager Is Always Available

Finally as I think about the thinking Christian woman and the need to offer encouragement, I am reminded of the many times Christ brought out the best in others, offering help and hope and giving of Himself over and over again. Remember the story of the Samaritan woman? The Word says he "must needs go through Samaria." (John 4:4.) Needs go? It was miles out of His way. Yet this has to be one of the most dramatic encounters in the Bible. I suppose it still shocks the extreme legalists of our day when they come across this account in John's Gospel. Somehow we'd rather disassociate Jesus from having anything to do with divorced people. But the Samaritan woman was a divorcée many times over!

In fact, she was at the very bottom of the scrap heap of humanity. She's been described as a seeking, seductive, lonesome, passionate woman of dalliance, a castoff of five men and living unmarried with a sixth. Apparently she had lost her faith in God and then, in an effort to fill up the void in her hungry heart, had made a shipwreck of her love life.

She came to draw water that day at high noon, more than likely in the midst of sweltering heat. Most people stayed indoors where it was cool, but not this woman. She came to the well at mid-day so as to avoid the contempt and scorn of the townspeople.

Jesus' approach to her, as it was to all unsaved individuals, was shaped by His desire to save her. *Everyone* needs to be shown the way into the kingdom of God. What a person is on the outside is not important. It is what he or she can become on the inside after an encounter with the living Christ that matters most.

Christ's conversation with this notorious woman, over the top of a well not more than four feet across, could have sparked a public scandal. Jesus didn't care. His compassion for her affords us a beautiful view of the pure grace of God. What an encouragement that encounter was to her! It changed her life, and the lives of the villagers as well.

I know many divorced women who have experienced ostracism, disapproval and harsh criticism from Christian friends (and even their relatives). One look at Jesus' treatment of this "scarlet woman" should be convincing proof of how we are to treat those who have gone through the trauma and heartache of a marriage that didn't work out. I was actually told by one brother in Christ that it would be better for me to end up in a mental institution than to get a divorce. Would Jesus have said that to the woman at the well?

What saved me from total despair? I encouraged myself in the Lord. His Word assured me that if I would be strong and of good courage, if I wouldn't be afraid, and if I would trust Him, He would be with me wherever I went, whatever I did (Deuteronomy 31:6).

If you need encouragement and it isn't forthcoming from anyone, get a good concordance and look up the many references to the word *courage*. I can assure you that you will be encouraged after you complete that study. You will have courage to spare, enough to share lavishly with others who desperately need it. Be an encourager!

When We Don't Feel Like Giving

Surely there must have been times when even the Son of God experienced fatigue. The Bible tells us He was like us, sin excepted, so that He could fully identify with us. During such weary times, Jesus withdrew from the ever-present crowds and called upon the Father for renewal. If it was necessary for Him, how much more so for us!

Oswald Chambers' writings have been an inspiration to me for years. In his classic, *My Utmost for His Highest*, he calls the death of Jesus the performance in history of the very Mind of God.

Jesus' death was the supreme example of caring. His death was the reason He came.

When we have discouraging moments, let us remember this demonstration of love. Can we do less than to expend ourselves for others in offering encouragement?

The thinking Christian woman cultivates caring qualities. One of the ways we show how much we care is by seeking to bring out the best in others and by being considerate. It is a small thing we can do. We aren't being asked to die.

I smile as I recall the many times my thinking Christian women friends have called me on the phone in response to the nudging of the Holy Spirit just to encourage me. I cannot finish this chapter without acknowledging such help. I think of blind Nancy in Houston who I have talked about in other books. Nancy and her mother Goldya are two of the greatest encouragers I've ever known. It's been incredible through the years to answer the phone and hear the two of them say, "We just felt led of the Lord . . . what's going on out there these days?" Inevitably those calls have come when I desperately needed to hear the Voice of Love speaking through them.

Then there is Barbara . . . Barbara Johnson from Southern California. What a supreme example of a thinking Christian woman! Barbara's calls have scraped literally hundreds of women, including me, off the ceiling more times than I care to remember. But that's Barb's special ministry. In fact, she calls it the "Spatula Ministry" because she herself has experienced what it's like to splash on the ceiling without "anyone to peel you off."[2]

And Anne Anderson (also mentioned in Chapter 4). Even though her health problems have been utterly draining, she picks up the phone when she senses God telling her to call with words of encouragement. Here is a woman who knows exactly what to say to bring out the best in others. Her care and consideration are exemplary.

We need to remind people from time to time, especially when the Holy Spirit brings someone to mind, that we love them and are thinking of them. Most important, we need to encourage one another with the knowledge that *God is faithful.*

When you don't feel up to offering the encouragement someone else may need, call upon the Father for His encouragement so you *can* be an encourager. Take time to "get apart" before you "come apart." The Bible provides a beautiful example in the character of David. When he was "greatly distressed," (1 Samuel 30:6), he "encouraged himself in the Lord his God" (KJV). The Encourager is always available.

Think on These Things...

Principle: The thinking Christian woman is an encourager. She seeks to bring out the best in others; she is a giver offering help and hope. She is considerate.

God's Word says, "If you have any encouragement from being united with Christ, if any comfort from His love, if any fellowship with the Spirit, if any tenderness and compassion, then make my joy complete by being like-minded, having the same love, being one in spirit and purpose... Each of you should look not only to your own interests, but also to the interests of others" (Philippians 2:1,2,4, NIV).

1. For your encouragement, who wrote the Gospel of Mark? Who is mentioned in 2 Timothy 4:11b? Does past failure need to disqualify us from present and future usefulness?
2. The Bible gives ample evidence that some people God used mightily would have been considered failures by today's standards. Pause and think who some of those people were. Does this encourage you?
3. Consider some of the ways you can be an encouragement to others. Make a list of what you will conscientiously seek to do in the days ahead.
4. Look up references to "courage" in a concordance. Share what you find.

Part V

The Thinking Christian Woman Never Gives Up; She Handles Her Emotions Intelligently

Hard times are made worse by low thinking.
—Roy L. Smith

The Christian who has dedicated his life to God and has shouldered his cross need not be surprised at the conflict in which he at once finds himself engaged. Such conflict is logical; it results from the nature of God and of man and of Christianity.
—A. W. Tozer[1]

I walk in the strength of the Lord God.
—Psalm 71:16 TLB

She Possesses Staying Power; She Is Committed and Courageous 𝄞

Wait on the Lord; Be of good courage, And He shall strengthen your heart; Wait, I say, on the Lord!
(Psalm 27:14)

I was standing in front of the mirror hurriedly putting on my makeup. The work was piled high on my desk—nothing new about that—and once again I was under the pressure of deadlines. Does it all sound familiar?

While your specific scenario may differ from mine, the stage is set. The thought and feelings that come tumbling in upon us are the same. *God, I can't handle much more of this! It's too much of too much! What am I going to do?*

How many times I have cried out like that! That particular morning it sounded like an echo. And then I heard the inner voice I have come to recognize as God speaking, *Don't panic! Haven't I always helped you?*

I had to smile. I was still on my feet. The momentary panic didn't stand a chance in the presence of such help.

I began to remember the many times God had helped me. Actually, there were times without number. "God is our refuge and strength, *A very present help in trouble*" (Psalm 46:1, italics added).

God is not an absentee Omnipotent. He is always available.

Principle

The thinking Christian woman never gives up; she has a conquering spirit. She possesses staying power, and is committed and courageous.

In speaking to a meeting of Christian artists in San Jose, California, on the disciplines needed to become accomplished in their field, I told them writing was work—aspiration, inspiration, frustration, isolation and perspiration. I shared that there were times I likened writing to walking up a hill backwards with my ankles tied together.

But I went on to encourage them. I spoke of the rewards, the sense of accomplishment, the rapport you establish with people—all the good things, the icing on the cake.

Afterwards I invited their questions and comments. I fully expected all sorts of inquiries about the practical aspects of getting published. But no, the first question was, "How do you handle the discouragement?"

"Yeah," another voice chimed in, "tell us more about climbing those hills. When you get to the top, what then?"

Mind Over Mood

The challenge of the hills will always be there, but we have a heavenly Father who knows all about climbing them. He is Lord of the hills, Lord of all the circumstances that come into our lives. The disappointments, the closed doors, the difficult people, the petty

irritations, the major catastrophes, the waiting, the un-
certainties, the lonely hours, the anxieties, the frustrations, the aspirations, the unfulfilled dreams, the anger
over perceived injustices, the inequities life seems to
dish out—all these and much more are known to the
Father. He understands. He cares.

I began by telling my questioners that discouragement is usually preceded by disappointment. If left un-
tended, that disappointment can lead to despair. However, we have been called to exercise *mind over mood*. I
pointed to the apostle Paul, who genuinely knew what
he was talking about when he wrote about the discouragement that is the all too common lot of man. He'd been
there. In fact, he was there at the time he wrote his
letters. His was no ivory tower speculation. It was "rub-
ber hitting the road" reality. He didn't write in an air-
conditioned office surrounded by self-help books. He
wrote to real people living in tough times while he
himself was in a rough spot. Have you ever tried writing
a letter from prison?

Perhaps your situation is a prison-like experience. If
so, Paul's words should take on added meaning. There is
help in the Word of God. Help and hope.

To be disappointed is to forget Romans 8:28, "And we
know that all things work together for good to those who
love God, to those who are the called according to *His*
purpose."

To be discouraged is to forget 1 Samuel 30:6, "Then
David was greatly distressed, for the people spoke of
stoning him . . . But David encouraged himself in the
Lord his God."

To despair is to forget 2 Corinthians 4:8, "We are hard
pressed on every side, yet not crushed; we are perplexed, but not in despair . . ."

"Oh, Timothy, my son," Paul wrote, "be strong with the strength Christ Jesus gives you" (2 Timothy 2:1, TLB). Here is the first key for dealing with discouragement. We find this call to *be strong* scattered from one end of the Bible to the other. That's why the Word is so practical and helpful in our hill climbing.

Perhaps Paul was remembering some of the Psalms as he wrote to Timothy. David and the other writers of Psalms wrote from the depths of human experience. As I look into my Bible, the Psalms are underscored, colored and dated—silent evidence that I've clung to them like a dying man clings to a life support system. I highly recommend the Psalms during your times of discouragement. When the enemy assails you, flinging his fiery darts seeking to destroy you, rush to the Word. God is your sanctuary.

In telling Timothy to be strong, Paul provided three illustration—a soldier, an athlete and a hard-working farmer. "Take your share of suffering as a good soldier of Jesus Christ . . . Follow the Lord's rules for doing His work, just as an athlete either follows the rules or is disqualified and wins no prize. Work hard, like a farmer who gets paid well if he raises a large crop. Think over these three illustrations," Paul said, "and may the Lord help you to understand how they apply to you" (2 Timothy 2:3,5-7, TLB).

As Paul instructed Timothy in this passage, he reminded him that in times of discouragement he was comforted by remembering that even though he was chained, "the Word of God is not chained." Even when we are too weak to have faith, God remains faithful to us and will help us (vv. 9-13). This is how we escape from Satan's trap (v. 26).

The key to overcoming discouragement and possessing staying power is to keep our thinking in tune with scriptural truth.

*Then we can make responsible choices because the principles of
the Word, not our emotions or our moods, will dictate our
responses to the hill climbing.*

It is a matter of mind over mood. Obedience is the
desired response. We listen, take heart, are encouraged,
trust and obey.

When I hear God say to David, "I want you to trust Me
in your times of trouble, so I can rescue you and you can
give Me glory" (Psalm 50:15, TLB), something in me cries
out, "Oh yes, dear Father, I hear You. I'm listening, I'm
obeying and I'm trusting You."

With the psalmist I repeat, "O Lord, don't hold back
Your tender mercies from me! My only hope is in Your
love and faithfulness. Otherwise I perish, for problems
far too big for me to solve are piled higher than my
head . . . My heart quails within me. Please, Lord, rescue
me! Quick! Come and help me! . . . Please don't delay!"
(Psalm 40:11-13,17b, TLB).

"Take courage, my soul! Why be discouraged and sad?
Hope in God! I shall yet praise Him again. Yes, I shall
again praise Him for His help . . . He is my help! He is my
God!" (Psalm 42:5,6a,11b, TLB).

The Father knows how to heal broken hearts and bind
up our wounds. He is a rescuer.

Conquering Through Christ

The names of a number of contemporary Christians
come to mind when I think of women who have demonstrated a conquering spirit. Corrie ten Boom, Mary
Crowley, Cathy Meeks, Mary Dorr, Lila Trotman, Mar-
ianna Slocum, Edith Schaeffer, Marj Saint Van Der Puy,
Nancy DeMoss and Barbara Johnson are just a few. These
thinking Christian women refused to give up on life

although each of them faced incredibly difficult experiences. They possessed staying power. They were committed and courageous, and never gave up.

Mary Dorr was determined to conquer flying so she could accompany her husband, a skilled pilot, and take over in case of an emergency. She kept the fact that she was taking lessons a secret and mastered the skill in time to give her husband the shock of his life when she wrapped her license and presented it to him as a gift one Christmas.

But then the unthinkable happened. Her husband, son and 10 businessmen flew into the wilds of British Columbia on a vacation trip. One day they decided to do some "lake hopping." Her husband was piloting the plane when he fell forward dead, the victim of a massive coronary. Mary, who knew how to fly, wasn't there. None of the businessmen knew how to fly. Her son Johnny in the copilot's seat had to take control of the plane. He knew he had to reach civilization, but even he didn't know how to fly. Then he remembered something his mother had once told him: "If you are in an impossible situation you don't say *if* I can do it, but you say I *can* do it and I'll be given the strength from the Lord."

Johnny prayed, and was able to safely land the plane at a little place called Prince George. Later Mary told him, "Johnny, I am very proud of you. Your faith saw you through. You cared enough to do what had to be done. We are our brother's keeper. You cared about your father and those men so much that you asked in faith, believing, and you received a miracle."

The conquering spirit that was so much a part of Mary Dorr was greatly needed in the weeks and years that lay ahead as she helped her family through multiple tragedies, including the loss of her son Denny just three years after her husband's death. "At times the agony was almost more than I could bear. Then I would remember that the Lord never gives us too heavy a burden, one we cannot carry if we believe in and trust Him," Mary once told me.

Thinking Christian Women Move Forward on Their Knees

There are many people who find it difficult to understand how one can move forward on her knees, or walk up a hill backward with her ankles tied together. Yet, that is just what Mary Dorr experienced.

"I cannot tell you how many times I had to go to my knees and cry out, 'God, I cannot go on alone! How can I meet all the bills and give these children the education they need?' But in the next breath, I was able to say, 'I will go on, I know You are supporting me in everything I am doing,' " she says.

Mary did the necessary, practical, at-hand things that had to be done. She sold everything. Her family adopted an entirely different lifestyle, scaled down so the children could receive their education and the family could survive financially. "While I was often overwhelmed at the responsibility of being both a mother and a father to our children, I did not despair. I knew that God was watching out for us," she explains.

Today Mary Dorr is recognized as the executive director of Religion in Media (RIM). That organization presents "Angel" awards for television programs, movies, radio shows, books and record albums based on excellence in production and high moral or religious content. What a great lady! A real thinking Christian woman.

Victor Hugo wrote, "Have courage for the great sorrows of life and patience for the small ones; and when you have laboriously accomplished your daily task, go to sleep in peace. God is awake."

How easily we forget that Jesus said, "In the world ye shall have tribulation."

The saintly Rutherford shouted in the midst of serious and painful trials, "Praise God for the hammer, the file and the furnace." How could he do that with such joyous abandon? The answer is that he loved the Master of the hammer, he adored the Workman who wielded the file and he worshiped the Lord who heated the furnace for the blessing of His children.

A. W. Tozer reminds us we are living in soft and carnal times. The attitude of a Rutherford doesn't find much sympathy among believers these days. Instead, we tend to think our Christian walk should be painless. What we want is to escape the penalty of past sins and get to heaven without too much suffering. Tozer notes, "The flaming desire to be rid of every unholy thing and to put on the likeness of Christ at any cost is not often found among us...

"The devil, things and people being what they are, it is necessary for God to use the hammer, the file and the furnace in His holy work of preparing a saint for true sainthood. It is doubtful whether God can bless a man greatly until He has hurt him deeply.

"Without doubt we of this generation have become too soft to scale great spiritual heights. Salvation has come to mean deliverance from unpleasant things. Our hymns and sermons create for us a religion of consolation and pleasantness. We overlook the place of the thorns, the cross and the blood. We ignore the function of the hammer and the file."[1]

I know, however, that the suffering many committed Christians are called upon to endure is not external. Often it involves inward pain, not necessarily visible to

others. Many of us fight inner battles of self-deprecia-
tion, despondency and loneliness. These struggles are
very real and I would not, for one moment, overlook
their painful reality.

We have one of two choices when confronted with the
"unthinkables of life." When the bottom board is knocked
out from under us we can either sit down on the thresh-
old of God's purpose and die of self-pity, or we can
affirm, like Job, "Though He slay me, yet will I trust
Him" (Job 13:15).

Think on These Things . . .

Principle: The thinking Christian woman never gives
up; she has a conquering spirit. She possesses staying
power and is committed and courageous.

God's Word says, "Wait on the Lord; Be of good courage,
And He shall strengthen your heart; Wait, I say, on the
Lord!" (Psalm 27:14).

Psalm 27 was my mother's favorite, and it has become
very meaningful in my life also. I can understand why
she, widowed at age 36 while pregnant with me and
having two other small children dependent on her, would
have found so much comfort, encouragement, help and
hope in this psalm. I would encourage you to read and
study its verses. It is a psalm of David, an exuberant
declaration of his faith.

Sometimes the circumstances of our lives thrust us into
what appears to be a desert of uncertainty or a swamp of
doubt and even cynicism. Our faith is sorely tested. At
such times we need to stake our claim in Christ and hold
on. Here are some steps you can take:

1. Dare to be specific with God and with yourself. Trust Him for victory in your experience (1 Corinthians 10:13).
2. Acknowledge there will be risks ahead, maybe even some failures. Certainly you will experience some doubts, difficulties, problems and setbacks. Hill climbing is tough work. Recognize that in this world we will not be exempt from tribulation (John 16:33).
3. Venture forth in faith to be God's woman where you are now. Submit to His will, and you will benefit eternally from His strength and grace (2 Corinthians 4:16-18).
4. Think through all your options—how you can maximize possibilities for present peace and future happiness and minimize pain and disappointment. Exercise the power of your mind.
5. Acknowledge that not all suffering is bad. I like what Catherine Marshall wrote, "The Gospel is truly good news. The news is that there is no situation—no breakage, no loss, no grief, no sin, no mess—so dreadful that out of it God cannot bring good, total good, not just 'spiritual good,' if we will allow Him to. Our God is the Divine Alchemist. He can take junk from the rubbish heap of life, and melting this base refuse in the pure fire of His love, hand us back—gold."[2]
6. In your particular "school of whatever," ask the Father to help you learn your lessons. James said the testing of our faith produces endurance, and if we will let endurance have its perfect work, we will be complete, lacking in nothing (James 1:2-4).
7. Read and meditate on these passages: Romans 5:3-5; Hebrews 2:10, 5:8.

She Values Inner Solitude: the Stilling of Her Heart before God and the Peace and Restfulness that Result ♪

> *Make it your ambition to lead a quiet life.*
> (1 Thessalonians 4:11, NIV)

> *Be still, and know that I am God.*
> (Psalm 46:10)

The need for solitude and quietness before God has never been greater than it is today. There are so many things to distract us and hinder quality thinking time. A. W. Tozer points out that one of the ways the civilized world destroys men is by preventing them from thinking their own thoughts.

The thinking Christian woman doesn't allow others to do her thinking for her. While she graciously listens to the counsel of others and knows the Bible says there is safety in a multitude of wise counselors (Proverbs 11:14), ultimately she bases her choices on what she knows is God-pleasing and what she senses He is saying to her. She has developed what I call the listening ear and the hearing heart. She is sensitive to God and knows the many ways He speaks to her.

Principle

The thinking Christian woman values inner solitude: the stilling of her heart before God and the peace and restfulness that result. She is a woman at peace with herself.

Such peace comes at a price. That price involves resting in the quiet assurance that God is in control of one's life. It requires centering one's thoughts on God, and being still so that encounters with Him can take place in the deepest part of one's being.

The thinking Christian woman's life is a statement that says Someone Else is in charge. Her life reflects quality control and inner stability that come from consistently *listening* to God.

A. W. Tozer said the heart seldom gets hot while the mouth is open. "A closed mouth before God and a silent heart are indispensable for the reception of certain kinds of truth. No [wo]man is qualified to speak who has not first listened."[1]

I am reminded of one 8-year-old's definition of thinking, "When you keep your mouth shut and your head keeps on talking to itself."

Progress in the Christian life is directly proportional to the time we spend growing in the knowledge of God and His Word. He responds to our efforts to know Him.

David wrote, "Mark this well: The Lord has set apart the redeemed for Himself. Therefore He will listen to me and answer when I call to Him. Stand before the Lord in awe . . . Lie quietly upon your bed in silent meditation. Put your trust in the Lord" (Psalm 4:3,4a,5, TLB).

The constant awareness of God's enfolding presence deepens as we cultivate our communication with Him, holding inward conversations with Him and worshiping Him in spirit and in truth. "Those who love Your laws have great peace of mind and heart and do not stumble ... O Lord, listen to my prayers; give me the common sense You promised. Hear my prayers; rescue me as You said You would ... Stand ready to help me because I have chosen to follow Your will ... let Your laws assist me" (Psalm 119:165,169,173,175b, TLB). In a world where there is so much that can trip us up and make us stumble in our faith, words like these stand out as beacon lights, beckoning us to come and learn more.

Twentieth century living could be summed up by stating that we are surrounded by persistent clamor and multiple distractions. How are we to hear the still, small voice above the din? The call to God's people today is to simplify our lives and make room for Him.

Brother Lawrence instructed: "Make your heart a spiritual temple, wherein you adore Him incessantly. Do not think or say anything that may displease Him."

We must develop a habit of the heart. Brother Lawrence spoke of the will as being master of the faculties. "Hold yourself in prayer before God like a paralytic beggar at a rich man's gate," he said. "Let it be your business to keep your mind in the presence of the Lord."

This faithful saint observed that practicing the presence of God does not bring fatigue to the body; on the contrary, it brings tranquility of soul. "Nothing in the world is more sweet and delightful than the kind of life that is in continual conversation with God. Only those who practice and experience this can comprehend what I mean."

He spoke of God as being the center, the place of rest in all circumstances. "Your example of walking in the presence of God will be a stronger inducement to others to do likewise than any arguments you can propose. Pray that your very countenance of a sweet and calm devotion will edify others. Even in the greatest hurry of business, you can preserve your recollection of God and your heavenly mindedness. You can work with an even, uninterrupted composure and tranquility of spirit. The time of business should not make you different from the type of person you are in prayer."[2]

Our responsibility then is to walk the road of God's choosing, to get close enough to Him that we can hear Him speaking to us in all situations. That is the tranquil life. The resting life. The life that has found peace.

Peace Rules the Day When Christ Rules the Mind

"Thou wilt keep him in perfect peace, whose mind is stayed on Thee: because he trusteth in Thee" (Isaiah 26:3, KJV).

Someone has said you can't control the length of your life, but you can control its width and depth. You can't control the contour of your face, but you can control its expression. You can't control the weather, but *you can control the atmosphere of your mind*. Why worry about things you *can't* control when the things you *can* control can bring blessed tranquility to your innermost being, peace and solitude beyond compare.

We don't come by this attitude easily, however. We are so prone to take matters into our own hands that resting comes hard for most of us.

The solitude I speak of isn't totally in keeping with the dictionary definition for the word. Webster defines solitude as the state of being solitary or alone; seclusion; isolation; remoteness; a lonely or secluded place.

Then why did I choose this word? Because it is an "inner solitude," an "aloneness with God and our thoughts," to which I refer. We need to seclude *our thoughts* so we can keep in tune with *His*. The isolation involves being in the world and part of all that's going on around us outwardly, but inwardly communing with the Father. *God, I need Your direction. Father, what do You think of this? Lord, I want to make the right decision in keeping with Your will. Father, give me Your guidance. Help, Lord!*

And this communication should take place not only in our times of need, but all throughout the day. Turning our thoughts to the blessedness, grace and mercy of the Lord is refreshing and revitalizing. To send up praise and adoration to Him, to thank Him for being Who He is and for what He has done. To say, *Thank You, dear Father, for Your love*—that is pleasing to the Father.

Think how much it means to you as a parent when one of your children calls just to say, "I love you, Mom." Just so, the "Father heart" of God thrills to hear our expressions of love.

If this kind of solitude is unfamiliar or new to you, let me urge you to begin nurturing a "habit of the heart" that spontaneously turns your thoughts heavenward. You can develop this habit like all other ones that are good for you. For example, you discipline yourself to leave salt out of your diet when the doctor says "high blood pressure." You forego anything sweet when he says "diabetes." When he tells you "exercise," you begin a program of walking, jogging, bicycling or whatever. Habits are formed by consistently doing what needs to be done. Likewise, you can foster the habit of the "burning heart," the heart that seeks the Father before anyone or doing anything else. It becomes like breathing. You can't survive without it.

This sweet inner communion with the Father was a blessed experience in the lives of many saints of the past whose life stories make for such inspiring reading. Thomas Kelly, in his classic *A Testament of Devotion*, explains it like this:

> There is a way of ordering our mental life on more than one level at once. On one level we may be thinking, discussing, seeing, calculating, meeting all the demands of external affairs. But deep within, behind the scenes, at a profounder level, we may also be in prayer and adoration, song and worship, and a gentle receptiveness to divine breathings.[3]

Henri Nouwen says, "We are called to solitude . . . in loving encounter with Jesus Christ. It is in this solitude that we become compassionate people. . . ."[4]

Finding Peace: Like a River Glorious

As I seek nourishment for my inner being, I find that old hymns such as "Like a River Glorious" bring real refreshing.

> Like a river glorious
>   Is God's perfect peace,
> Over all victorious
>   In its bright increase;
> Perfect yet it floweth
>   Fuller every day,
> Perfect yet it groweth
>   Deeper all the way.
>
> Chorus:
> Trusting in Jehovah,
>   Hearts are fully blest—

Finding, as He promised,
Perfect peace and rest.

Hidden in the hollow
Of His blessed hand,
Never foe can follow,
Never traitor stand.
Not a surge of worry,
Not a shade of care,
Not a blast of hurry
Touch the spirit there.[5]

Those words ring so true. The spirit in communion with the Father possesses resources the world cannot comprehend. Peace and rest come as a result.

Peace seems so elusive these days. I can easily despair as I look at the world around me, read the paper and watch the evening news. Do you feel that way too at times?

How then can we live in peace? The answer is, by rightly ordering our thoughts. David recognized that God understood his thoughts afar off. He could pray, "Search me, O God, and know my heart; test my thoughts. Point out anything you find in me that makes you sad, and lead me along the path of everlasting life" (Psalm 139:23,24, TLB).

Jesus knows the thoughts of our hearts. Earlier in this book I referred to Jesus taking a little child and setting her in the midst of his squabbling disciples, who were arguing about who was going to be the greatest, because He "perceived the thoughts of their heart" (Luke 9:47).

It is God who works the miracle of transformation in our hearts so we can possess His divine attributes, including His peace. Years ago I read about F. B. Meyer, the 19th century preacher whose writings are still read and savored. In recounting an experience with unruly and noisy children, the writer tells how he was driven to claim from the Savior the gift of His own gentle patience:

> "Thy patience, Lord!" and instantly so divine a calm filled his spirit that he realized that he had made a great discovery. And from that moment he had retained the extremes of his brief petition, inserting between them the grace, the lack of which was hurrying him to sin. In moments of weakness, "Thy strength, Lord!" or in moments of conscious strength, "Thy humility, Lord!" When assailed by unholy suggestions, "Thy purity, Lord!" or when passing through deep waters of trial, "Thy resignation and restfulness, Lord!"[6]

Reading that passage and then hearing Dr. J. Vernon McGee speak on this subject years ago when I was a young and very busy wife and homemaker revolutionized my thinking. I found myself calling out those words when I desperately needed patience, strength and love. After doing so, I would experience an incredible awareness that what I was asking for would come. I was fortified in my place of inner solitude, and my lapses into doing things in my *own* strength became fewer and fewer.

Think with Your Heart

A. W. Tozer calls attention to a writer (name unknown) who warned that it may be fatal to "trust in the squirrel-work of the industrious brain rather than to the piercing vision of the desirous heart."

Have you ever observed a squirrel hard at work? I recall sitting in our Fort Worth, Texas, home watching squirrels gather pecans that had fallen from the trees in our backyard. They were so industrious. It was fun to peer out at them from my study window.

But we are not to be like that in our thinking. The busy work of the brain can take its toll. For example, sleepless nights that occur when the brain refuses to turn off can result in burnout. Uncontrolled thinking can play havoc with our adrenal glands.

Understanding that the excessive busywork of our brains causes stress and thereby produces severe wear and tear on our bodies points out how vital it is for us to take control of our thinking processes. The apostle Paul repeatedly stressed the need to replace our destructive emotions with positive ones. That's why we need a place of inner solitude. We must discipline our minds to bring them under the control of the Holy Spirit. To still our minds (hearts) before God is to allow Him to bring peace into the midst of our stressful situations.

The Greek church father, Nicephorus, taught that we should learn to think with our hearts. "Force your mind to descend into the heart," he wrote, "and to remain there . . . When you thus enter into the place of the heart give thanks to God and, praising His mercy, keep always to this doing, and it will teach you things which in no other way will you ever learn."[7]

He continues, "Christianity must embrace the total personality and command every atom of the redeemed being. We cannot withhold our intellects from the blazing altar and still hope to preserve the true faith of Christ."[8]

Paul wrote, "Pray without ceasing" (1 Thessalonians 5:17). When we learn that this *is* possible, that the heart can be turned toward God even during the busyness of our days, we will never again want to be deprived of His comforting, empowering Presence.

The invitation has been extended, "Come to me, all you who are heavily burdened, and I will refresh you" (Matthew 11:28, author's paraphrase). Only Jesus can give the kind of refreshment we need for our over-burdened souls. He moves in with tenderness to restore the psyche. "Be still," He gently says, "and know that I *am* God" (Psalm 46:10).

We are called to embrace Him in faith and then rest in divine love. Such "restedness" will enable us to intersect with the world as servants of Christ.

"Keep thy heart with all diligence; for out of it are the issues of life" (Proverbs 4:23, KJV).

Think on These Things . . .

Principle: The thinking Christian woman values inner solitude: the stilling of the heart before God and the peace and rest that result.

God's Word says, "Be still and know that I *am* God" (Psalm 46:10).

"Make it your ambition to lead a quiet life" (1 Thessalonians 4:11).

"Thou wilt keep him in perfect peace, whose mind is stayed on Thee; because he trusteth in Thee" (Isaiah 26:2, KJV).

1. The principle referred to in the above verses calls for a disciplined thought life. Read and meditate on Matthew 15:18 and Luke 6:45.
2. Ask yourself, "What kind of a thinker am I?"
3. Here is a partial list of the kinds of damaging thoughts we think. Do they apply to you? Add others that are unique to your situation.

Unwanted thoughts
Critical thoughts
Irrational thoughts
Negative thoughts
Defeatist thoughts
Self-destructive thoughts
Vain thoughts
Doubting and indecisive thoughts

4. Explore Scripture and see what verses you can find that will help you change your thought patterns. Try writing specific verses next to some of the negative thought patterns listed above. Next time you find yourself reverting to wrong thought habits, think of these verses.

5. Would you say your thoughts turn immediately to God when you are confronted with decisions? Do your thoughts turn to Him often during the day just in praise and thanksgiving?

Christ-like behavior begins as a Christ-like thought. The way we respond to what life holds out to us begins with how we think.

Part VI

The Thinking Christian Woman Is Good to Herself

Live as you will wish to have lived when you come to die.

Your life is like a book. The title page is your name; the preface your introduction to the world. The pages are a daily record of your efforts, trials, pleasures, discouragements, and achievements. Day by day your thoughts and acts are being inscribed in your book of life. Hour by hour, the record is being made that must stand for all time. Once the word "finis" must be written. Let it then be said of your book that it is a record of noble purpose, generous service, and work well done.

—Grenville Kleiser

Whatever a man sows, that he will also reap.
—Galatians 6:7

Commit your works to the Lord,
And your thoughts will be established.
—Proverbs 16:3

She Takes Charge of
Her Health

> *Do you not know that you are a temple of God, and that the Spirit of God dwells in you? If any man destroys the temple of God, God will destroy him, for the temple of God is holy, and that is what you are. Let no man deceive himself.*
> (1 Corinthians 3:16-18a, NAS)

Everyone wants to go to heaven, but no one wants to die. We want to live forever. Moreover, we want to live our entire lives as beautiful women; we don't want to grow old and age. How can you age without growing old?

People today are spending a lot of time, money and effort searching for the legendary "fountain of youth." The media bombard us with images of "beautiful people" and products guaranteed to produce results for us. No one wants to get old as we generally think of it . . . with sagging muscles, brittle bones, a cantankerous personality and a senile mind.

Also, we are scared to death of *flab*. I've observed, as I'm sure you have, that almost every magazine on the newsstand offers some new diet, some "proven weight loss plan." It is a sure guarantee of sales. People have been and are making fortunes on weight loss clinics, as well as seminars and books on exercise and diet. What are we to make of all this?

Many years ago I experienced a very serious health problem. My thinking about keeping slim and attractive had obliterated my better judgment. In addition, I had a floundering marriage and was a busy wife, mother, writer and businesswoman.

My children recall finding me rolling on the floor in my living room, holding my stomach doubled over in pain. Finally the doctor put me in the hospital. "Duodenal ulcers," he said after looking at the X-rays.

"Young lady, why are you doing this to yourself?" he asked. He was a fine Christian doctor. Looking me straight in the eye he added, "Don't you know your body is the temple of the Holy Spirit? You aren't treating it right..."

Following that encounter, yet another incident forced me to face the fact that I had to take charge of my health. While I was being treated for the ulcers, my children were not allowed to come into the hospital room. One day when my husband brought them to the window I overheard my youngest child Kraig say, "Oh look, my mama's in there alive!" I was overwhelmed and grieved to think I had brought this worry on my little children, so much that the youngest feared I was no longer alive.

The Turning Point

I cried out to God and begged for His help. I promised that if He would heal me I would never again neglect my body like that. What had happened to me?

I realized I had allowed the "gods of this world" to invade my thinking. Totally immersed in my own problems, a self-centered preoccupation with my body had led me to the brink of losing my health. In the process I had brought anguish and much concern to my family. And I knew I was grieving the heart of God. That acknowledgment was the turning point.

Some of you may also be grieving the Father-heart of God in the way you are treating your body. Moreover, you are causing your loved ones a great deal of concern.

"Do you not know that you are a temple of God, and that the Spirit of God dwells in you?" the apostle Paul wrote. "If any man destroys the temple of God, God will destroy him, for the temple of God is holy, and that is what you are. Let no man deceive himself" (1 Corinthians 3:16-18a, NAS).

Principle

The thinking Christian woman takes charge of her health. She knows her body is not her own. "For you were bought at a price; therefore glorify God in your body and in your spirit, which are God's" (1 Corinthians 6:20).

"For you are God's temple, the home of the living God, and God has said of you, 'I will live in them and walk among them, and I will be their God and they shall be my people' " (2 Corinthians 6:16b, TLB).

Following my return home from the hospital, I made an appointment to see Gladys Lindberg, a woman who has been a pioneer in the field of health and nutrition and is founder of and nutrition consultant for the Lindberg

Nutrition Service in Southern California. When God gives us insight into a matter, I have found He often wants us to take the practical, near-at-hand steps that are needed. He expects us to do our part. This in no way diminishes His miracle-working power; He can and does in some cases heal people instantly. But sometimes He chooses to work through medical professionals. I knew about Mrs. Lindberg, so I made and kept the appointment.

When I met with her, she graciously explained the need to nourish my body, that the way to stay healthy, energetic and attractive was to take care of my cells. "Cell function is the basis of all life. As each of us grows older, our trillions of body cells gradually change. The best way to maintain health and vitality is to keep these cells performing in harmony," she said smiling kindly.

I marveled at this lovely woman's poise and serenity. I knew she was older than she looked because I knew she had a daughter about my age. Yet she looked at least 20 years younger.

I remember commenting about her youthful appearance and that I couldn't help wondering how she had achieved this. "Aging is not senility and poor health, young lady," she responded. "These are conditions generally brought on by chronic malnutrition and inattention to what the body needs to maintain good health and vigor at *any* age."

I was irresistibly attracted to her and what she had to say. I hadn't stopped to think about health in those terms before. Mrs. Lindberg outlined a comprehensive program for me to follow, and God used her to help me regain my health. The result was renewed energy and a zest for living.

"Living on This Side of Disease"

When people come to Gladys Lindberg for a consultation they are, she explains, looking for health. "People are living on 'this side of disease,' " she says, "in the twilight zone of health."

She believes people fail to understand the delicate ecological balance God created within their bodies. They also fail to understand the role of nutrition, and unknowingly deprive themselves of optimum health. These imbalances, left uncorrected, frequently lead to more serious disease. Recognizing subtle deviations from good health and taking steps to correct them early is preventive medicine at its best. This is *taking charge of your health*. We ourselves often hold the key to preventing serious illness.[1]

"It is never too late to start over," Gladys says. "A new beginning is possible at any age, at any time. Preventive medicine places most of the care of your body into your own hands. We cannot hold our doctors responsible for our health—or for our lack of it. Their responsibility is to help us when we are sick. They are involved in what is called 'crisis medicine.' That is what they are trained for, and we should be thankful we can call upon them in times of need.

"Nor can we expect the government to look after our health. The government does what it can to control communicable diseases and to reduce pollutants in our water and air, but it is our personal responsibility to learn what contributes to illness and break whatever bad habits we may have acquired. If we hope to prevent disease and untimely aging, what we really need is more respect for the human body. This can lead to a longer life cycle—certainly one more active and happy,"[2] she states.

Listen to Your Body Talk

Out of that experience of dealing with my health crisis came the realization that I needed to listen to my body talk. We've been reading and hearing about body language for years—the way we sit, move, gesture with our hands—but that's not what I'm referring to. I discovered my body would tell me when it wasn't up to par.

I began to ask myself questions: "Why are you having a headache? What did you have for lunch? Oh, you haven't had lunch. No wonder you've got a headache." My body was saying, "Feed me. Give me some protein." Maybe it was trying to tell me it needed a big glass of water.

I now keep mental track of my eating and drinking habits so that when my body signals me, I can analyze why it is behaving a certain way. For instance, if I forget to take my calcium supplement with regularity, the cramps in my legs let me know I've been negligent. In this and other ways I've become familiar with my body and I am in a much better position to take charge of my health. The results are worth the discipline required.

The apostle Paul wrote, "Let every one be definite in his own convictions . . . The truth is that we neither live nor die as self-contained units. At every turn life links us to the Lord and when we die we come face to face with Him. In life or death we are in the hands of the Lord. Christ lived and died that He might be the Lord in both life and death . . . It is to God alone that we shall have to answer for our actions" (Romans 14:5, 7, 12, Phillips). Yes, even in matters pertaining to how we have treated our bodies.

Think on These Things...

Principle: The thinking Christian woman takes charge of her health. She knows she has been bought at a price; her body is not her own.

God's Word says, "Do you not know that you are a temple of God, and the Spirit of God dwells in you? If any man destroys the temple of God, God will destroy him, for the temple of God is holy, and that is what you are. Let no [wo]man deceive himself [herself]" (1 Corinthians 3:16-18a, NAS).

1. Be ruthlessly honest with yourself and ask, "How am I treating my 'temple'?"
2. List those things you are doing to your body that you know are injurious to your health.
3. What are you going to do about this? Can you honestly claim to be a thinking Christian woman and go on abusing your body and neglecting your health? Here are some steps you can begin to take immediately:

a. Get serious with yourself and with God. Admit your weakness(es) and implore God's help. Commit yourself to a disciplined program to regain what has been lost through self-indulgence and lack of will power (won't power).
b. Read a good book or books on health and nutrition, but this time don't just give mental assent to what you are reading. Study what is being said, apply it to yourself and search for information that will benefit and help you. In addition to Mrs. Lindberg's book, *Take Charge of Your Health*, I recommend Emilie Barnes' and Sue Gregg's book, *Eating Right*.

c. Give yourself some assignments. For example, "Today I will write down everything I eat and look up the caloric value." Surprise! The next day say to yourself, "Today I will seek professional help," if that is required. If you cannot afford such help, at least consult your doctor and follow the cutback program for weight loss control he can outline for you. If your problem is smoking, he can help with that also, or he can refer you to someone who can.

I know many woman who have done marvelously on Weight Watchers. In fact, everyone I've asked recently about how they've lost weight has attributed it to that program.

Neva Coyle's "Overeaters Victorious Program" is also highly motivational. It addresses not only overeating, but other discipline problem areas as well. For additional information write: Neva Coyle, P. O. Box 179, Redlands, California 92373 (mention that you read about her program in this book). Neva turned her life over to God and then applied the principles of the Word to herself. The result was a 100-pound weight loss and the discovery of a way to live free.

Whatever you do, determine that with God's help today you will take charge of your health. Be a thinking Christian woman in this area of your life as well.

She Exercises Discernment; She Guards Her Tongue; She Is Enthusiastic, a Joy-filled Woman of Faith, and Has a Zest for Living 🎵

> *Give to Your servant an understanding heart*
> *... that I may discern between good and evil.*
> (1 Kings 3:9)

> *Set a guard, O Lord, over my mouth; Keep a*
> *watch over the door of my lips.*
> (Psalm 141:3)

> *The joy of the Lord is your strength.*
> (Nehemiah 8:10)

> *And whatever you do, do it heartily, as to the Lord*
> *and not to men.*
> (Colossians 3:23)

A friend's child, in trying to capture a bird for a pet, accidentally killed it. Upon viewing the dead bird a younger child in the family sorrowfully asked, "Where does the song go?"

Even so, where does the song go when you and I wound someone with bitter words? When tongue-lashings are our weapon, what happens to another's song?

How many times have we stabbed others verbally by defending ourselves? Does what we say take the song

149

away from those we least desire to hurt?

The wounds of life leave scars. Must we add to them?

--------------------------------- ❀ ---------------------------------

Principle

The thinking Christian woman exercises discernment; she guards her tongue. With David, she knows the value of praying, "Set a guard, O Lord, over my mouth; Keep watch over the door of my lips" (Psalm 141:3).

--------------------------------- ❀ ---------------------------------

James 1:26 has a warning for us as we think about our speech, "Anyone who says he is a Christian but doesn't control his sharp tongue is just fooling himself, and his religion isn't worth much" (TLB).

Many of us go through life hampered by the stereotypes that are hung upon women in general. In particular, I believe we Christian women get stuck with these labels more often and have a more difficult time shaking them than our secular counterparts.

In their book, *What Every Woman Still Knows*, authors Mildred Cooper and Martha Fanning question whether we should actually try to get rid of the stereotypes. They say stereotypes are usually based on truth, and it's not the truth we want to get rid of, only the erroneous feelings people have about it. As this relates to the stereotype that women talk too much—that we are gossipers and the oft-implied suggestion that we could be more discerning—what are we going to do?

This presents a challenge for the thinking Christian woman. If there is power in words, and who can deny there is, let us seek to use our word power wisely.

The Dearth of Discernment

Our society desperately needs discerning, thinking Christian women. There is no question in my mind that we are experiencing a dearth of discernment today because we as Christians have been brainwashed to think that to be discerning is the opposite of love—that somehow we should be awash in a sea of love without ever expressing *any* kind of criticism or suggestion.

As an example of this, I think of the heartbreak and confusion that accompanies church splits. We recently witnessed the departure of several fine Christian families from a certain church. These were discerning people —loyal, loving, long-time supporters of the work of the church in their community—who had been trying for some time to bring about what they felt were needed changes. They were exercising what they believed were their God-given critical faculties, but they weren't doing it in a troublesome way.

They were genuinely concerned for what they felt to be a deteriorating condition, and hoped to help bring about a renewal of spiritual life. One of the men lovingly expressed his views before the church trustees, and another wrote his thoughts in a letter. Afterward, one woman in the church called them "accusers of the brethren" and another said they were under the devil's influence. Finally, rather than be the cause of division in the church, these committed Christian families quietly left one by one.

Paul prayed for the Philippian church that their love might abound more and more *in knowledge and in all judgment,* that they might approve things that are excellent (Philippians 1:9,10). The Bible says to "judge with righteous judgment" (John 7:24b).

Our "gift of gab" can be one of our greatest assets, but surely not if we fail to exercise discernment. Of the Proverbs 31 woman it is said, "When she speaks, her words are wise, and kindness is the rule for everything she says" (v. 26, TLB). The Preacher wrote that the words of a wise [wo]man's mouth are gracious (Ecclesiastes 10:12). The thinking Christian woman is careful to exercise discernment in many different areas of her life.

Avoiding Spiritual Hypocrisy

Author Oswald Chambers cautions about becoming spiritual hypocrites, focusing our discernment on criticizing others instead of on praying for them. He says: "Take heed lest you play the hypocrite by spending all your time trying to get others right before you worship God yourself."[1]

The secret to avoiding this trap is to become an intercessor instead of a criticizer. This will still the tendency to gossip and to let our tongues get out of control. Discernment is God's call to intercession, never to faultfinding.

Another area in which discernment is vital is in maintaining a right perspective. Chambers says, "Be careful to maintain strenuously God's point of view, it has to be done every day, bit by bit; don't think on the finite. No outside power can touch [this] viewpoint . . . We are not in God's showroom, we are here to exhibit one thing—the absolute captivity of our lives to Jesus Christ."[2]

The way to overcome the all too common tendency to tenaciously hang on to our own point of view is to determine to know the will of God. Jesus said the path of blessing lies in doing and saying what we know is in keeping with His teachings (John 13:17).

The counterfeit of obedience is mistaking our ardor for discernment. Let us be sure we know the will of God.

Finally, discernment is vital when it comes to our roles in others' lives. A Texas father once told me one of the most difficult things he had to learn to do was back out of his adult children's lives. "They were looking to me to supply all the answers to their problems; they weren't learning how to look to and depend on God," he shared.

I've had to learn that too. Such learning doesn't come easy, especially when we see our children headed for potential problems.

Yet whether it's our husbands, children or friends, business acquaintances, whoever . . . we are well advised not to interfere in what God is attempting to show someone else. Sometimes we put our hand right in front of God's permissive will as it relates to what He wants to get across to that person.

The thinking Christian woman will be careful lest she gets in God's way. She will ask for discernment so that blessing, help and learning can result for all concerned. Let us take care not to regard ourselves (or let others think of us) as amateur "divine providences."

Solomon's Example

Solomon's example says much to the discerning woman. When God appeared to Solomon in a dream the young king was told, "Ask! What shall I give you?"

Solomon responded by saying he felt like a little child in contrast to his father David whose throne he had inherited. Yet his request to God was so wise! "Therefore give to Your servant an understanding heart to judge Your people, that I may discern between good and evil" (1 Kings 3:9).

God was pleased. And He took into account what Solomon did *not* ask for: a long life for himself, riches, the lives of his enemies.

We will be wise to take note of what pleased God about Solomon's request. How much we, too, need God's wisdom. How much the world around us needs what we can share as a result of having His understanding. Let us make Solomon's prayer our own. We can be assured God will answer it.

"If you want better insight and discernment," Solomon said, "and are searching for them as you would for lost money or hidden treasure, then wisdom will be given you, and knowledge of God Himself; you will soon learn the importance of reverence for the Lord and of trusting Him.

"For the Lord grants wisdom! His every word is a treasure of knowledge and understanding. He grants good sense to the godly—His saints. He is their shield, protecting them and guarding their pathway. He shows how to distinguish right from wrong, how to find the right decision every time. For wisdom and truth will enter the very center of your being, filling your life with joy" (Proverbs 2:3-10, TLB).

Enthusiasm, Joy, Strong Faith and Zest for Living

Ralph Waldo Emerson said, "Every great and commanding movement in the annals of the world is a triumph of enthusiasm." He called enthusiasm the mother of effort, for without it nothing great was ever accomplished.

I learned an important lesson on the need for enthusiasm many years ago (see chapter 7), and would call to your attention once again the apostle Paul's words, "And whatever you do, do it heartily, as to the Lord and not to men" (Colossians 3:23). We are "to do" with enthusiasm. Other translations and paraphrases use words such as: work hard and cheerfully; work at it with all your heart, as working for the Lord, not for men; work as from the soul; put your whole heart and soul into it.

Imagine what could be accomplished in our generation if we as thinking Christian women grasped the full implication of these words. Narrow it down . . . think of what could be accomplished in your community, your church, your neighborhood, your home and your personal experience if wholehearted enthusiasm, strong faith and zest for living characterized your life!

Kindling the Fire

A. W. Tozer's writings pronounce a heavy indictment on Christians who arrange their lives so as to profess Christianity without being affected by its implications. He says, "To many Christians, Christ is little more than an idea, or at best an ideal; He is not a fact. Millions of believers talk as if He were real and act as if He were not. And always our actual position is to be discovered by the way we act, not by the way we talk."[3]

Tozer refers to a pseudo belief, lacking in enthusiasm for the things of the Lord. He says, "There is an evil which I perceive under the sun . . . It is the glaring disparity between theology and practice among professing Christians."[4]

He speaks of it as a "wide gulf that separates theory from practice in the church," so much so that an inquiring stranger who chances upon both would scarcely dream there was any relation between them. We must ask ourselves, "Where is our commitment, our holy zeal? Where is the outworking of our faith in actual experience, our enthusiasm for God's Word?"

It is impossible to kindle a fire in someone else's heart until it is burning in our own.

Principle

The thinking Christian woman is enthusiastic, a joy-filled woman of faith who has a zest for living.

Marked by Joy

Let us return to a principle first discussed in chapter 1, that of being child-like. How exuberant children can be when they are doing what interests them most! What fun and excitement they convey!

Look also at their beautiful faith. How trusting and accepting they are! How sweet are their questions as they ask about Jesus and God.

And then there is the unbridled enthusiasm, joy and appreciation children demonstrate when they receive something special. I think of our grandchildren and the fun we had recently giving them much-wanted teddy-bears. Giggles, squeals and happy smiles clearly showed their thankfulness and excitement as they discovered the contents of the brightly wrapped packages.

As Christians, we should exemplify the child-like traits of enthusiasm, faith, joy and thankfulness. After all, we ought to be the happiest, most enthusiastic people in the world.

The original meaning of the word "enthusiasm" is "supernatural inspiration or possession" (to be possessed by God). We have been redeemed by the blood of Christ, His love has forgiven our past, His peace will guard our present and His will can be ours both now and in the future as we entrust ourselves to His guiding.

Moreover, as His children, we have the promise of an eternity with Him.

In his refreshing book, *Laughter, Joy and Healing,* Donald E. DeMaray speaks of enthusiasm and joy as Siamese twins. "One cannot move without the other. The two can be either quiet or outgoing in manner, but they will create enthusiasm. When the Spirit of God is the Author of that enthusiasm and joy, they set hearts afire, and in that flame mere words are translated into reality. And that is communication."[5]

Real joy is not just a "ha-ha" kind of feeling that lasts only for a time. While it is sometimes expressed in fun-loving smiles and laughter, there is more to it than that. True joy is the abiding inner peace and happiness that comes from knowing God. It's not dependent on circumstances, and it runs far deeper than mere emotion. In essence, it is the outward expression of God's presence and power in our lives.

One of the most joy-filled women of faith I know is Barbara Johnson, who I mentioned in Chapter 9. She *knows* what it's like to have true joy, anchored not in circumstances but in Christ. You see, Barb lost one son in Vietnam, another was killed by a drunk driver and she then discovered her third son had opted for a homosexual lifestyle.

Yet out of all that heartache she founded "Spatula Ministries," to "scrape people off the wall," as she says, when they go through traumatic experiences. She publishes a newsletter filled with things to make her readers smile, and suggests everyone start a "Joy Box" of cartoons, jokes or anecdotes to bring out when we need a smile.

After surveying the contemporary scene or dealing with the hard times life has to offer we may wonder if there is anything left to smile about. An undue preoccupation with the concerns of daily living can quickly deplete our lives of joy. At this point we run the risk of becoming "sour saints." "Sourness," however, is never synonymous with "saintliness."

It's interesting to note that unripe fruit is always bitter. Joy is the second fruit Paul lists in Galatians 5:22 where he talks about what our lives should be producing.

In Psalms David wrote, "I will be glad and rejoice in You" (Psalm 9:2). Notice the *I will*. Joy is a choice. As thinking Christian women, we *always* have something to smile about. As Psalm 119:111 says, ". . . Thy testimonies . . . are the joy of my heart" (NAS).

Think on These Things . . .

Principle: The thinking Christian woman exercises discernment; she guards her tongue; she is enthusiastic, a joy-filled woman of faith and she has a zest for living.

God's Word says, "Therefore, give to Your servant an understanding heart . . . that I may discern between good and evil . . ." (1 Kings 3:9).

1. God told Solomon, "Ask for anything you want." Solomon asked for discernment and wisdom, an understanding mind. Would you have answered that way?
2. Remember the childhood rhyme, "Sticks and stones can break my bones, but words can never hurt me"? Well, it's not true. Words do hurt, often far more than we realize. Are you asking God to guard your tongue?
3. Meditate on the meaning of *true* joy. Based on that definition, are you a joy-filled woman of faith who has a zest for living?

Part VII

The Thinking Christian Woman Recognizes the Hand of God Upon Her Life

Not *was*, not *may be*, nor *will be*. "The Lord *is* my shepherd," *is* on Sunday, *is* on Monday, and *is* through every day of the week; *is* in January, *is* in December, and every month of the year; *is* at home, and *is* in China; *is* in peace, and, *is* in war; in abundance, and in penury.

—J. Hudson Taylor

For I know the thoughts that I think toward you, says the Lord, thoughts of peace and not of evil, to give you a future and a hope.

—Jeremiah 29:11

She Sees Herself as a God-Planned Individual 𝄪

> *Don't let the world around you squeeze you into its mold, but let God re-make you so that your whole attitude of mind is changed.*
> (Romans 12:2, Phillips)

> *For I know the plans I have for you, says the Lord. They are plans for good and not for evil, to give you a future and a hope.*
> (Jeremiah 29:11, TLB)

You are a divine original. God-planned. Unique. A one-of-a-kind masterpiece. God saw you before you were born; He planned all your days.[1] You are His workmanship.[2]

Do you see yourself that way? Not all women do. In fact, the more I read, the more I am convinced the struggle with a poor self-image is universal. It's a problem that causes many people great anguish, and it might surprise us to know who some of those individuals are.

When I did the interviews for my book *Living Cameos*, I was taken aback when Shirley Dobson, wife of the much-respected Dr. James Dobson, told me she had struggled with a poor self-concept for many years. Her difficulties stemmed from childhood, as is true for many of us.

While sources for our depression and feelings of inferiority may vary, they have many similarities. The emotional apathy that results is a recurring fact of life. Dr. Dobson calls this condition "The D's." "The majority of adult females seem to experience times of despair, discouragement, disinterest, distress, despondency and disenchantment with circumstances as they are,"[3] he says.

During an interview with Bev LaHaye, founder of Concerned Women for America, I discovered she, too, had been plagued by fears and insecurities for years. She told me it was not until she realized she was a special creation from God's own hand that she was able to break free of those negative feelings.

That realization is vital to changing the way we view ourselves. It is only as I remember that I am a God-planned woman, that I am special to my heavenly Father and that He has the details (yes, even the minute details) planned for me, that I can handle my own feelings of inadequacy.

Knowing Who We Are

The thing that has helped me most in seeing myself from God's perspective is knowing the Bible repeatedly declares that we as His children are the crowning glory of His creation. The psalmist speaks of looking at the heavens, the work of God's fingertips, and then asking, "What is man that You are mindful of him? And the son of man, that You visit him?" (Psalm 8:4).

He answers these questions by saying, "You have made him a little lower than the angels. And You have crowned him with glory and honor: You have made him to have dominion over the works of Your hands..." (vv. 5,6).

I was fortunate to grow up in a home where the Bible was read at every meal. Mother kept it on a small shelf under the kitchen table, and mealtimes weren't complete until she'd fed us from the Word of God. I knew I was a child of God. The Bible said so.

I also learned as a small child that my daddy was in heaven with God. God was my Heavenly Father. I felt special to Him, and I can remember boasting to my little friends, "My daddy is with God." In my mind's eye, I would crawl up into God's lap whenever I was sad, hurt or lonely. There I felt comforted, loved and accepted. I would even go to sleep at night with my hand outside the blanket so God could hold it. I had an incredible awareness that God was near.

As I grew older, the tendency to compare myself to others was always there. From the moment we step into our first school classroom we are part of a competitive environment, and we have to learn to deal with that. Unfortunately some people never do.

We find ourselves feeling "too skinny," or "too fat," "too smart" or "not smart enough." We don't usually attach names to these feelings when we are young, but later we find ourselves experiencing them again—the inadequacy, the failure, the doubt. We perceive ourselves as inadequate human beings.

It's a vicious cycle. One moment we feel good about an accomplishment; the next we are down in the pits because we failed to achieve. We look at another person, someone God may have specially gifted in a certain way, and we feel our own competency to be woefully lacking.

What is the remedy? Is there one?

Even though I knew I was special to God as a child, self-doubt began to haunt me as I grew into young womanhood. It was only as I retreated into the Bible that I could regain my sense of identity—that I felt valued and that God had gifted me, too. The key was seeing that I was nothing apart from my heavenly Father. My true value lay in my relationship to Him.

Ephesians 1, for instance, says we are accepted in the Beloved (v. 6). Chapter 2 affirms that we are His workmanship, created in Christ Jesus for good works (v. 10). All that we are is based on *givens* from God. If we can accept that fact, we can be free to acknowledge our limitations and enjoy our successes because we know it is all of Him.

The apostle Paul urged Timothy to, "Be diligent to present yourself approved to God, a worker who does not need to be ashamed, rightly dividing the word of truth" (2 Timothy 2:15). We can depend on God to actualize all we are meant to be when we diligently give our all to Him. This is where we find our true value. Anything apart from that is unfulfilling.

I have been so blessed and helped in my spiritual pilgrimage by the daily devotional book, *Streams in the Desert*. Written by Mrs. Charles Cowman, it has taught me many important lessons, including the fact that to be unhappy with myself is to show discontent. God is my Maker. Consequently, feelings of not liking myself are surely not from Him. I have had to reckon with the all-too-obvious fact that someone else is constantly trying to drag me down, and that someone is Satan.

The apostle Paul said, "I have learned in whatever state I am, therewith to be content" (Philippians 4:11). I have had to label my feelings of discontent as "sin," and deal with them as such.

Heart's-ease

Author Cowman tells the story of a king who went

into his garden one morning and found everything with-
ered and dying. He asked the oak that stood near the
gate what the trouble was. He found it was sick of life
and determined to die because it was not tall and beautiful like the pine. The pine was all out of heart because it
could not grow grapes like the vine. The vine was going
to throw its life away because it could not stand erect and
produce as fine a fruit as the peach tree. The geranium
was fretting because it was not tall and fragrant like the
lilac, and so on through the garden.

Coming to a heart's-ease, he found its bright face lifted
as cheery as ever. "Well, heart's-ease, I'm glad, amidst
all this discouragement, to find one brave little flower.
You do not seem to be the least disheartened."

"No, I am not of much account, but I thought that if
you wanted an oak, or a pine, or a peach tree, or a lilac,
you would have planted one; but as I knew you wanted a
heart's-ease, I am determined to be the best little heart's-
ease that I can."

> Others may do a greater work,
>   But you have your work to do;
>   and no one in all God's heritage
>   Can do it as well as you.

Mrs. Cowman points out that those who give their
lives to God without reserve are in every state content,
for they will only what He wills and desire to do for
Him whatever He desires them to do.[4] I often have to remind myself of that quaint little story and say to myself,
"Helen, be a heart's-ease."

--- ---

Principle

The thinking Christian woman sees herself as a God-planned individual. She believes the Lord will work out His plans for her life (Psalm 138:8). This motivates her to seek what the Bible calls "the more excellent way" (1 Corinthians 12:31).

--- ---

The More Excellent Way

In recent years, a whole spate of "excellence" books has appeared in the marketplace. One of the most popular has been *In Search of Excellence*, which analyzes America's best-run companies. The widespread acceptance of this book and the impact it has made on our generation's thinking indicates the concerns and aspirations of society. We want to be successful, well-liked, attractive, intelligent and whatever else fits our definition of "excellent."

The idea of excellence has its origins in Scripture. The Scriptural definition, however, includes an element of love not often considered by the world. When Paul wrote to the Christians at Philippi, he began by reminding them of his confidence in them and that God, who began a good work in them, would continue it (Philippians 1:6). Following that statement, he plunged into a discourse on love—that it might abound more and more, and extend to its fullest development in knowledge and all keen insight (v. 9). He then returned to excellence:

"... so that you may approve the things that are excellent, in order to be sincere and blameless until the day of Christ..." (v. 10, NAS).

Paul gave his stamp of approval to pursuing excellence, but not at the expense of hurting others nor in disregard for first of all excelling in love.

The Amplified Bible explains the meaning of the word *excellent* like this: "... learn to sense what is vital, and approve and prize what is excellent and of real value—recognizing the highest and the best, and distinguishing the moral differences; and that you may be untainted and pure and unerring and blameless, that—with hearts sincere and certain and unsullied—you may [approach] the day of Christ, not stumbling nor causing others to stumble" (v.10).

Webster's dictionary defines *excel* as, "to be superior or preeminent in good qualities or praiseworthy actions." *Excellence* is, "the possession chiefly of good qualities in an unusual degree; surpassing virtue, merit, worth, value."

Value. Do you feel valuable to God? To others? To yourself? You can, and moreover, you should. The unique combination of your insights and abilities, your personality and potential, have been molded by God Himself. You are not "less" than any other woman, or your husband or any other male (as so many in the Christian world would have us believe). When God made you, He saw you were "excellent," and of value.[5]

A Proper View

As we begin to understand our "excellence" in Christ, we are able to view ourselves correctly. As a result, we are less likely to be squeezed into the world's mold, thinking as they think and responding as they respond. We have a new perspective that enables us to sift through what the media bombard us with daily, messages that say we need to do this, to acquire this or become like this or that to be acceptable. If we try to be conformed to the world's standard, we are sure to be unhappy and discontented.

So often we set ourselves up for failure and unhappiness. And the older we get, the more devious are the devil's attempts to influence our thinking. We look at our lives, the aspirations and dreams we once had, and begin to feel unfulfilled. Why do you think there are so many marriages that fall apart at mid-life? The mid-life crisis is not just a figment of the imagination. It happens.

We look at others whose accomplishments (looks, clothes, houses, possessions) outshine ours and we begin to despair. If our thinking is controlled by the desire to have what we don't have, or to have more and/ or better possessions, then the perishable things of this world can block out the "more excellent" judgment God wants us to exercise.

Paul referred to that judgment when he wrote, "Don't cherish exaggerated ideas of yourself or your importance, but try to have a sane estimate of your capabilities by the light of the faith that God has given to you all" (Romans 12:3, Phillips).

Others may not value you as highly as you deserve. But God does. And you can.

Possessing a healthy self-image is simply thinking honestly about yourself. It's an inside measurement of who you would be without Christ in your life and who you are because of Him.

Where do we learn this kind of perspective? From God and His Son. The Father showed how much He loved us by giving His Son; the Son showed how much He loved us by giving His life. To selflessly love like that—loving yourself in obedience to the Word and focusing your thoughts on others—is to choose the way of blessing, the more excellent way.

"I know the plans I have for you . . ."

Mother used to say to me, "God has plans for your life. Don't run ahead of Him."

As I reflect on her wise counsel and the many times I failed to heed it, I am forced to admit that the greatest heartaches in my life have come as a result of running ahead of God, taking matters in my own hands rather than praying and waiting for the inner peace He provides to give direction on a given matter.

What then is our role in directing our lives? Are we nothing but human puppets being manipulated by a Divine Omnipotent?

The answer is no. We can and should make plans. The difference for the thinking Christian woman, however, is that she knows the final outcome is in God's hands.[6] She accepts that with confidence and patience.

One night recently when sleep evaded me I recalled Jeremiah 29:11, "I know the plans I have for you, says the Lord. They are plans for good and not for evil, to give you a future and a hope."

These were not unfamiliar words. I had heard them and even recited them to myself on numerous occasions. They had become, in fact, watchwords for my life. Signposts. Guiding lights. Wisdom from the Father.

What God has promised, He will do. He can be taken at His Word. After thinking on these precious verses, I turned over and slept peacefully.

We are God-planned individuals. To accept that is to enjoy an inner assurance that provides stability through all the vicissitudes of life. "Reverence for God gives a man deep strength; his children have a place of refuge and security; Reverence for the Lord is a fountain of life" (Proverbs 14:26,27a, TLB).

Wherever this finds you—whether greatly unsettled by circumstances or deeply damaged in your feelings of confidence—please hear the conclusion of the matter from our Maker himself.

You *are* a one-of-a-kind Designer original, of value to Him. You are loved. Believe this, and trust yourself to the God who made you, for He will never fail you (1 Peter 4:19, TLB).

> The Lord will work out His plan for your life [for my life, for our lives] for His lovingkindness continues forever (author's paraphrase of Psalm 138:8).

As singer Ethel Waters was so fond of saying, "God don't make no junk!"

Think on These Things...

Principle: The thinking Christian woman sees herself as a God-planned individual. She believes the Lord will work out His plan for her life (Psalm 138:8). This motivates her to seek what the Bible calls "the more excellent way" (1 Corinthians 12:31).

God's Word says, "For I know the plans I have for you, says the Lord. They are plans for good and not for evil, to give you a future and a hope" (Jeremiah 29:11, TLB).

"Do not think of yourself more highly than you ought, but rather think of yourself with sober judgment" (Romans 12:3a, NIV).

Consider these thoughts from Shirley Dobson. "Healing and fulfillment come as you look beyond yourself. I am often reminded of 2 Corinthians 5:7 where we are told that we are to walk by faith, not by sight. I know this is true. It is the best way to be aware of who I really am—I'm a child of God. I've been created by Him as a unique individual.

"God doesn't want us to compare ourselves to others—to what they have or how they look. He accepts us as we are! And the past need not limit the present or the future. If we let Him, He will help us to forget the painful memories and overcome the struggles of a difficult childhood. He certainly did that for me . . . Everything good in my life today has resulted from His lovingkindness in my hour of need."[7]

1. Stop and think about your life. Have you approved the things that are excellent (Philippians 1:10)? Can you say of yourself: "I am of value; I am a woman of worth"? What is your potential value compared with your perceived value at this moment? In what way(s) do you sense you need to change or improve?
2. Do you see your life as God-planned? If so, what are specific areas you feel God may be nudging you to bring *more* under His control? If you don't see your life as God-planned, why not? Read the following Scriptures: Philippians 3:12-14; Hebrews 4:12-16; Matthew 6:25-34; 2 Corinthians 12:9; 1 John 3. What insights can you glean that can help you recognize your value?

She Sees God in Everything. She Lives Her Faith, Has a Thankful Heart and Trusts and Obeys God.

Look at the birds of the air, for they neither sow nor reap nor gather into barns; yet your heavenly Father feeds them. Are you not of more value than they?
(Matthew 6:26)

Be anxious for nothing, but in everything by prayer and supplication, with thanksgiving, let your requests be made known to God; and the peace of God, which surpasses all understanding, will guard your hearts and minds through Christ Jesus . . . And my God shall supply all your needs according to His riches in glory by Christ Jesus.
(Philippians 4:6,7,19)

It is never easy to come to the concluding chapter of a book and try to determine how to best finish. In my heart I know there is much more that could and should be said. I know, for instance, that I haven't pointed you sufficiently in the direction of the Proverbs 31 woman, but I think of what my friend Jeanne Hendricks said, "God wants to write a sequel to Proverbs 31 with us in mind. He has already given us the pattern to follow and has also furnished us with the 'how to.' 'If any [wo]man is in Christ, [s]he is a new creature; the old things passed

173

away; behold new things have come' (2 Corinthians 5:17)."[1]

Don't be too hard on yourself as you review what has been written and you think about where you have been, where you are and the direction it appears life is taking you. Be patient toward that which is unsolved in your life. As thinking Christian women we must recognize and remember that God *is* in everything. Diamonds don't happen overnight, and Rembrandt didn't paint by number. We are in process; we're not finished products. Give yourself time. Give God time.

I remember reading about a sign in a businessman's office that said, "You are not what you think you are. What you think you are."

Thinking is hard work.

Which brings us back to the original premise of this book, "As a [wo]man thinks in her heart, so is she" (Proverbs 23:7).

When Paul said we were to think Christ's thoughts and have His mind, he was not giving us an impossible assignment. Granted sometimes our circumstances leave us feeling hemmed in, our thinking all askew. We long for a release button that could somehow free us. Yet we do have such a release . . . in fact, Someone who can and will provide it.

"Therefore, since we have a great high priest who has gone through the heavens, Jesus the Son of God, let us hold firmly to the faith we profess. For we do not have a high priest who is unable to sympathize with our weaknesses, but we have one who has been tempted in every way, just as we are—yet was without sin. Let us then approach the throne of grace with confidence, so that we may receive mercy and find grace to help us in our time of need" (Hebrews 4:14-16, NAS).

What Is the Set of Your Sail?

Either our focus is heavenward,
or it is earthbound.
One ship drives east and another drives west
With the selfsame winds that blow;
'Tis the set of the sails
And not the gales
Which tells us the way to go.
—Ella Wheeler Wilcox

As A. W. Tozer insists, it's not how we *feel* but what we *will* that determines our spiritual direction. The call, then, is to set our sails to the will of God. When we do, we will find ourselves moving in the right direction no matter which way the wind blows.

As we look at Jesus' life, we see that He never got into a panic. There was a calm, consistent strength about Him in all situations. If we are to have the mind of Christ, then why is that quality so noticeably absent in many Christians' lives?

The book of Jude supplies the answer. We cannot display this inner peace unless we are building ourselves up in our most holy faith, praying in the Spirit (v. 20). This is how we maintain our life with God, refreshing ourselves so we can walk transformed and renewed in Him.

Oswald Chambers points to Peter walking on the water. That was easy, he says, compared to walking on dry land as a disciple of Jesus Christ day in and day out. Peter walked on the water to get to Jesus, but he followed Him afar off on the land. The truth of that observation hits home as Chambers notes:

We do not need the grace of God to stand crises; human nature and pride are sufficient. We can face the strain magnificently; but it does require the supernatural grace of God to live 24 hours in every day as a saint, to go through drudgery as a disciple, to live an ordinary, unobserved, ignored existence as a disciple of Jesus. It is inbred in us that we have to do exceptional things for God; but we have not. We have to be exceptional in the ordinary things, to be holy in mean streets, among people and this is not learned in five minutes.[2]

Failing to Accept God's Gifts

On a recent visit to Southern California we took gifts to our grandsons, David and Andrew. David's gift was really meant for Andrew as well, but each had to have something to open. Because David's gift was also part of his birthday present, it was a little larger in size. We explained that it was supposed to be shared with Andrew, then gave Andrew his present—a darling yellow felt stuffed bird. But Andrew was none too happy. He took one look at the bird, looked at me, and before we knew what was happening, POOF, it was flying through the air. I glanced up just in time to see it coming as I held up my hand to catch it.

Often we react the same way to the "gifts," the sometimes difficult experiences, God entrusts to us. We rebelliously throw them back in His face with complaining, discontent, anger and many other unlovely responses which are so much a part of our old nature and temperaments. We fail to see God in everything. Yet, we are told not to throw away our confidence which holds promise of a great reward.[3]

Hannah Whitall Smith talks about this principle in her classic, *The Christian's Secret of a Happy Life*. She speaks of earthly cares as being heavenly discipline. She calls them God's chariots sent to take the soul to its high place of triumphs (chariots that may be disguised as sufferings, trials, defeats, misunderstandings, disappointments and unkindnesses). Our trials may look like "Juggernaut cars of misery and wretchedness, which are only waiting to roll over us and crush us into the earth. But could we see them as they really are, we should recognize them as chariots of triumph in which we may ride to those very heights of victory for which our souls have been longing and praying. The Juggernaut car is the visible thing; the chariot of God is the invisible,"[4] she says.

Smith says we should pray that our spiritual eyes may be opened so we can see *all* the events of life, whether great or small, joyful or sad, as chariots for our souls. It is up to us, she adds, to choose whether we will allow these chariots to roll over and crush us or whether we, like Elijah, will climb up into them and let them triumphantly carry us onward and upward into "heavenly places."

Trust and Obey

Having this kind of attitude undoubtedly calls for an incredible amount of trust. Here we must return to a principle repeated many times in this book, being childlike as we look into the face of Jesus. Responding with wholehearted trust, nothing held back.

If we are to embrace this attitude, it is vital for us to see God as a *good and loving Father*. A loving father does what is ultimately best for his children. A good father does not willingly deprive them of that which will strengthen and nourish them; he wants them to live in joy and happiness. As Jesus said, "If you then, being evil, know how to give good gifts to your children, how much more will your Father who is in heaven give good things to those who ask Him" (Matthew 7:11).

The thinking Christian woman cultivates such a view of God. This thinking colors her life with confident acceptance, enabling her to trust and obey Him even in the hard times.

I have always had a strong faith in the goodness of my heavenly Father. This confidence came as a gift, for I never had the example of a loving earthly father. He died of cancer a few months before I was born.

Did my mother lash out at God for this? Was she bitter, angry or disillusioned with God for this? No. Rather, she taught me the song that was her life's theme, "Trust and obey, for there's no other way, to be happy in Jesus, than to trust and obey."[5] She consistently demonstrated trust in God and His faithfulness to her and her fatherless children.

Yes, I insist that my childhood without an earthly father was God's gift to me. Knowing myself as I do, I am sure I would never have developed the kind of God-consciousness and Christ-confidence I now have if I had not known so much deprivation and sorrow early in life.

Out of my experience of not having an earthly father I saw, even as a small child, that God was in everything. And although my behavior and attitudes today may not always demonstrate my belief, I always eventually come around and say, "I have deep faith, I trust my Father."

The banner that flies over my life is Psalm 56:3 and 4,

Whenever I am afraid
I will trust in You.
In God (I will praise His word),

In God I have put my trust;
I will not fear.

The thinking Christian woman lives her life in abiding consent to God's will and unwavering trust in His love. That mind-set gives her the restful, peaceful life that so many people, including Christians, are longing and searching for.

God is faithful. I commend you to His trustworthy care.

Thou wilt keep him [her] in perfect peace,
Whose mind is stayed on You.
Because he [she] trusts in You.
(Isaiah 26:3)

Yes, "Trust in the Lord forever, for in YAH, the Lord, is everlasting strength" (v. 4).

Think on These Things...

Principle: The thinking Christian woman sees God in everything. She lives her faith, has a thankful heart and trusts and obeys God.

God's Word says, "Look at the birds of the air, for they neither sow nor reap nor gather into barns; yet your heavenly Father feeds them. Are you not of more value than they?" (Matthew 6:26).

"Don't worry about anything; instead, pray about everything; tell God your needs and don't forget to thank Him for His answers. If you do this you will experience God's peace, which is far more wonderful than the human mind can understand. His peace will keep your thoughts and your hearts quiet and at rest as you trust in Christ Jesus" (Philippians 4:4-7, TLB).

1. Read and meditate on the above verses. Jesus' words in Matthew 6 and 7 provide tremendous insights on living as thinking Christian women. The idea that we are of more value to Him than the birds has always been special to my child-like heart. It's easy to remember, and I am reminded of it often during the day when I see the birds flitting about. What do these words mean to you in your present circumstances?
2. Is it difficult for you to see God in everything? Write out your feelings. Then in an act of trust lift them to the Father and say, "Dear Father, I give these thoughts to You. I do want to trust and obey You. I do want to see You in everything. Help, Thou, my unbelief."
3. I don't know what your particular circumstances may be, but I do know no one is exempt from doubting or wondering at times because of the trying situations that come into their lives. Consider how the following words may apply to you. Perhaps you will want to add your own "ings."

God In Our "Ings"

God is in our
loving,
our conceiving,
birthing,
our
going and our coming,
sitting and our rising,
sighing and our crying,
wondering and our whying,
moaning and our groaning,

He's in our
choosing,
trying and our failing,
complaining and our railing.
In our
serving and our sharing,
walking and our running,
He both precedes and follows.
When we're
helping,
waiting, wavering,
suffering,
grieving,
Yes, He's there.
You'll find Him in your
worshiping
praying,
trusting,
caring, laughing, singing,
There He is.
Wishing, wanting, longing.
Hoping, believing.
"Lo," He says, "I am with you always..."
Living or dying...
"Do not be afraid, nor be dismayed,
for the Lord your God is with you wherever
you go."

"This Thing Is from Me"

"My child, I have a message for you today. Let me whisper it in your ear, that it may gild with glory any storm clouds which may arise and smooth the rough places upon which you may have to tread. It is short, only five words, but let them sink into your inmost soul. Use them as a pillow upon which to rest your weary head. *This thing is from me.*

"Have you ever thought of it, that all that concerns you concerns Me, too? For, 'He that toucheth you, toucheth the apple of mine eye' (Zechariah 2:8). You are very precious in My sight (Isaiah 43:4). Therefore, it is My special delight to educate you.

"I would have you learn when temptations assail you and the 'enemy comes in like a flood,' that this thing is from Me, that your weakness needs My might, and your safety lies in letting Me fight for you.

"Are you in difficult circumstances, surrounded by people who do not understand you, who never consult your taste, who put you in the background? This thing is from Me. I am the God of circumstances. Thou camest not to thy place by accident; it is the very place God meant for thee.

"Have you not asked to be made humble? See then, I have placed you in the very school where this lesson is taught. Your surroundings and your companions are only working out My will.

"Are you in money difficulties? Is it hard to make ends meet? This thing is from Me, for I am your purse-bearer and would have you draw from and depend upon Me. My supplies are limitless (Philippians 4:19). I would have you prove My promises. Let it not be said of you, 'In this thing ye did not believe the Lord your God' (Deuteronomy 1:32).

"Are you passing through a night of sorrow? This thing is from Me. I am the Man of Sorrows and acquainted with grief. I have let earthly comforters fail you, that by turning to Me you may obtain everlasting consolation (2 Thessalonians 2:16,17). Have you longed to do some great work for Me and instead have been laid on a bed of pain and weakness? This thing is from Me. I could not get your attention in your busy days and I want to teach you some of My deepest lessons. 'They also serve who only stand and wait.' Some of My greatest workers are those shut out from active service, that they may learn to wield the weapon of all-prayer.

"This day I place in your hand this pot of holy oil. Make use of it freely, My child. Let every circumstance that arises, every word that pains you, every interruption that would make you impatient, every revelation of your weakness be anointed with it. The sting will go as you learn to see Me in all things."[6]

"This is from Me," the Savior said,
As bending low He kissed my brow,
"For One who loves you thus has led.
Just rest in Me, be patient now,
Your Father knows you have need of this,
Tho' why perchance you cannot see.
Grieve not for things you've seemed to miss.
The thing I sent is best for thee."

Then, looking through my tears, I plead,
"Dear Lord, forgive, I did not know,
'Twill not be hard since Thou dost tread,
Each path before me here below."
And for my good this thing must be,
His grace sufficient for each test.
So still I'll sing, "Whatever be
God's way for me is always best."[7]

Notes

Part I

1. A. W. Tozer, *The Knowledge of the Holy* (New York: Harper & Row, 1961), p. 52.

Chapter 1

1. "Take Time to Be Holy," William D. Longstaff, 1822-1894. Hope Publishing Co., used by permission.
2. Evelyn Christenson, *Lord, Change Me* (Wheaton, IL: Scripture Press, 1987), p. 97.
3. Andrew Murray, *The Inner Life* (Springdale, PA.: Whitaker House, 1984), pp. 63-64.

Chapter 2

1. Harry Blamires, *The Christian Mind* (Ann Arbor, MI: Servant Books, 1963), p. 132.
2. Ibid., p. 132. This book by Blamires is an excellent source for further reading on the subject of thinking Christianly. The thoughts expressed in this paragraph are a distillation of his material in the chapter entitled "Its Acceptance of Authority."
3. Ibid., p. 156.
4. Bill Hull, *Right Thinking* (Colorado Springs, CO: NavPress, 1985), p. 72.
5. Ibid., p. 72.
6. Andrew Murray, p. 120.
7. Tozer, p. 122.

Part II

1. A. W. Tozer, *The Set of the Sail* (Camp Hill, PA: Christian Publications, 1986), p. 60.

Chapter 5

1. J. B. Phillips, *New Testament Christianity* (London, England: Hodder & Stoughton, 1956), p. 112.

Part III

1. Tozer, *The Set of the Sail*, p. 93.
2. Tozer, *The Knowledge of the Holy*, p. 52.

Chapter 6

1. Tozer, *The Knowledge of the Holy*, pp. 52-53.
2. Martha Reapsome, *A Woman's Path to Godliness* (Nashville, TN: Thomas Nelson Publishers, 1986), p. 187.
3. John White, *The Golden Cow* (Downers Grove, IL: Inter-Varsity Press, 1979), p. 61.

Part IV

1. Anne Ortlund, *Disciplines of the Beautiful Woman* (Waco, TX: Word Books, 1977), p. 96.
2. Tozer, *The Set of the Sail*, p. 59.

Chapter 8

1. Amy Carmichael, *If* (Grand Rapids, MI: Zondervan Publishing House, 1972).

Chapter 9

1. William Barclay, *The Letter to the Hebrews*, *The Daily Study Bible* (Edinburgh: The St. Andrew Press, 1955), pp. 137-138.
2. Barbara's story is told in my book *Living Cameos*, and in her two books: *Where Does a Mother Go to Resign* and *Fresh Elastic for Stretched-Out Moms*.

Part V

1. A. W. Tozer, *Of God and Men* (Harrisburg, PA: Christian Publications, 1960), p. 61.

Chapter 10

1. Tozer, *The Root of the Righteous* (Camp Hill, PA: Christian Publications, 1986), pp. 136-137.
2. Catherine Marshall, *Something More* (New York: McGraw-Hill Book Company, 1974), p. 7.

Chapter 11

1. Tozer, *The Set of the Sail*, p. 15.
2. These excerpts are from a compilation of the writings of Andrew Murray and Brother Lawrence by Louis Gifford Parkhurst, Jr., entitled *The Believer's Secret of the Abiding Presence* (Minneapolis, MN: Bethany House Publishers, 1987).
3. Thomas Kelly, *A Testament of Devotion* (New York: Harper, 1941), p. 124.
4. Henri Nouwen, "The Desert Counsel to Flee the World," *Sojourners*, June 1980, p. 18.
5. Frances R. Havergal (1836-1879), "Like a River Glorious."
6. F. B. Meyer, *Christian Living* (New York: Revell, 1892), pp. 13-14.

7. A. W. Tozer, *God Tells the Man Who Cares* (Harrisburg, PA: Christian Publications, 1970), in the chapter entitled "We Need Sanctified Thinkers," p. 102.
8. Ibid., p. 103.

Chapter 12

1. Glady Lindberg and Judy Lindberg McFarland, *Take Charge of Your Health* (New York: Harper & Row, 1982), p. 4.
2. Ibid., p. 147.

Chapter 13

1. Oswald Chambers, *My Utmost for His Highest* (New York: Dodd, Mead & Co., 1963), p. 91.
2. Ibid., p. 298.
3. Tozer, *The Root of the Righteous*, p. 49.
4. Ibid., p. 51.
5. Donald E. DeMaray, *Laughter, Joy and Healing* (Grand Rapids, MI: Baker Book House, 1986), p. 150.

Chapter 14

1. Psalm 22:9 and Psalm 139:13-18.
2. Ephesians 2:10.
3. James Dobson, *What Wives Wish Their Husbands Knew About Women* (Wheaton, IL: Tyndale House Publishers, Inc., 1975), p. 15.
4. Mrs. Chas. E. Cowman, *Streams in the Desert* (Grand Rapids, MI: Zondervan Publishing House, 1925, 1950), pp. 7-8.
5. The reference is to Genesis 1:31. While that refers to original creation, I am convinced that as God formed each of us in our mother's womb, and as we were given life and breath, He looked at us, and declared us "excellent," too, and of value—great value.

6. Proverbs 16:1.
7. From personal interview.

Chapter 15

1. Jeanne Hendricks, *A Woman for All Seasons* (Nashville, TN: Thomas Nelson Publishers, 1977), p. 184.
2. Oswald Chambers, *My Utmost for His Highest*, p. 295.
3. The reference is to Hebrews 10:35.
4. Hannah Whitall Smith, *The Christian's Secret of a Happy Life* (Old Tappan, NJ: Fleming H. Revell Co., 1962), p. 227.
5. "Trust and Obey," James H. Sammis and Daniel B. Towner.
6. Mrs. Chas. E. Cowman, *Streams in the Desert*, pp. 35-36.
7. Ibid., pp. 36-37.

Other Good
Harvest House Reading

MORE HOURS IN MY DAY
by *Emilie Barnes*

There can be more hours in your day when you use the collection of calendars, charts, and guides in this useful book on home time management.

THE GRACIOUS WOMAN
Developing a Servant's Heart Through Hospitality
by *June Curtis*

June shares the secret of being a gracious woman and shows how to become the gracious woman God intended.

THE SPIRIT-CONTROLLED WOMAN
by *Beverly LaHaye*

This bestselling book gives the Christian woman practical help in understanding herself and the weaknesses she encounters in her private life and in her relationships with others. Told from a woman's point of view, this book covers every stage of a woman's life.

THE SEXUAL WOMAN
by *Joseph Mayo, M.D.* and *Mary Ann Mayo*

This provocative book clearly examines the many physical, emotional, and spiritual considerations relevant to the sexuality of today's Christian woman. Women will gain a thorough understanding of their unique physical makeup, the various physiological stages of their lives, and their everyday concerns related to sexuality. Drawing on their combined backgrounds in medicine and counseling, the Mayos offer an inspiring and informative look at every facet of a woman's identity and the unique responsibilities of the Christian woman regarding sexuality.

QUIET MOMENTS FOR WOMEN
by *June Masters Bacher*

Though written for women, this devotional will benefit the entire family. Mrs. Bacher's down-to-earth, often humorous experiences have a daily message of God's love for you!

Dear Reader:

We would appreciate hearing from you regarding this Harvest House nonfiction book. It will enable us to continue to give you the best in Christian publishing.

1. What most influenced you to purchase *The Thinking Christian Woman*?
   - ☐ Author
   - ☐ Subject matter
   - ☐ Backcover copy
   - ☐ Recommendations
   - ☐ Cover/Title
   - ☐ _____

2. Where did you purchase this book?
   - ☐ Christian bookstore
   - ☐ General bookstore
   - ☐ Department store
   - ☐ Grocery store
   - ☐ Other

3. Your overall rating of this book:
   ☐ Excellent   ☐ Very good   ☐ Good   ☐ Fair   ☐ Poor

4. How likely would you be to purchase other books by this author?
   - ☐ Very likely
   - ☐ Somewhat likely
   - ☐ Not very likely
   - ☐ Not at all

5. What types of books most interest you?
   (check all that apply)
   - ☐ Women's Books
   - ☐ Marriage Books
   - ☐ Current Issues
   - ☐ Self Help/Psychology
   - ☐ Bible Studies
   - ☐ Fiction
   - ☐ Biographies
   - ☐ Children's Books
   - ☐ Youth Books
   - ☐ Other _____

6. Please check the box next to your age group.
   - ☐ Under 18
   - ☐ 18-24
   - ☐ 25-34
   - ☐ 35-44
   - ☐ 45-54
   - ☐ 55 and over

Mail to: Editorial Director
Harvest House Publishers
1075 Arrowsmith
Eugene, OR 97402

Name _____

Address _____

City _____ State _____ Zip _____

Thank you for helping us to help you in future publications!